30 Days in Rome

One Month That May Change Your Life

Ken Hinkley

authorHOUSE®

AuthorHouse™
1663 Liberty Drive
Bloomington, IN 47403
www.authorhouse.com
Phone: 1 (800) 839-8640

New International Version (NIV)
Holy Bible, New International Version®, NIV® Copyright
©1973, 1978, 1984, 2011 by Biblica, Inc.® Used by
permission. All rights reserved worldwide.

Published by AuthorHouse 02/13/2017

ISBN: 978-1-5246-7092-4 (sc)
ISBN: 978-1-5246-7091-7 (e)

CONTENTS

INTRODUCTION

I am not much of a traveler. I have never been overseas to another nation to visit, let alone to be immersed in its culture. But I don't have to in order to understand the transition from living in an ungodly culture to one of living a life pleasing the God who saved me. That's what the letter to the Roman church is all about. The author (in this book I will assume it is Paul, based on what I believe to be sufficient evidence) tries to get new Christians to understand what it is like to live a vastly different lifestyle than they were used to. All around them there was human depravity, open sensuality, lack of morals, and a general lack of concern for the welfare of individuals. It was like the description given in the Old Testament where it was said that "everyone did what was right in his own eyes" even though it was a far cry from what God expected of them. Now as children of the heavenly King, they were expected to live a radically different way. As they struggled to be different, they had to regularly (and often) do a self-check to see that they were not being pulled back into the old way of living.

As you read each daily reading, try to see the parallels between what was happening in their situation and what is happening in your world. They faced many of the same struggles and temptations that you do. The advice given to them is equally applicable to your situation today.

A total of thirty lessons are in this series. Each one will be discussed separately so you can read them in the order given or you may select specific ones according to the topic under discussion. However, as you do so, try to keep in mind the main point of Paul's letter is that as a Christian reader you need to be sure you are living within the principles of Christ-like behavior, not as the rest of the world.

CHAPTER 1

A Preacher's Delight

Today's Bible Reading: Romans 1:1-17

I am not ashamed of the gospel because
it is the power of God for the salvation
of everyone who believes: first for
the Jews, then for the Gentiles.
For in the gospel a righteousness from
God is revealed, a righteousness that
is by faith from first to last, just as it is
written: 'the righteous will live by faith.'
—Romans 1:16, 17

I believe people in every profession have a dream or goal. There is something they would really love to do as the most glorious thing their profession offers. For a golfer it might be to play in a world tournament. For an architect, it might be to design a building that would attract millions of people and have his or her name attached to that building. For those who like to travel it might be to visit a particular country or place in the world just to say, "I've been there. I know now from experience what it's like to be there." For different people it would be different things. Perhaps you have a dream relating to your career or profession.

It's no different for pastors, teachers, and preachers of the Word. We, too, have things we would like to do, places we would like to go and say, "I was there. I visited such and such a church. I was there at a certain place at a certain time." Or we may have ministry goals that we would really like to achieve before the Lord asks us to step aside to make way for the next generation.

Paul points out, I think, three things in this passage that would be a preacher's delight. First, he says it's a preacher's delight to be a spokesman for God (vv. 1-6).

Paul, as we know, was an apostle appointed directly by Jesus Christ to be an ambassador for Him and to establish the church in those early days. He was to be instrumental in that. We know he was not the only one, for there was Peter and the other apostles who were declared by Christ to be apostles. Paul's primary mission was to the non-Jewish people. He refers to the Gentiles several times in these verses as the ones he wished to address.

He is a servant of Jesus Christ, he says. That means it should be a preacher's delight to have a servant attitude as a teacher or preacher. We need to have an attitude like that of Christ himself, who when He was on earth declared, "I came not to be served, but to serve others" (Mark 10:45). As by example, He washed His own disciples feet, implying that this is the way we should lead; by being there to meet the needs of those who have needs and by being ready to do what needs to be done for the ministry and for the cause of Christ, even if it means setting aside our pride or setting aside the things that we would like to do and doing what needs to be done instead.

Then we have in Acts where the deacons were appointed to distribute the food. Now, we think of deacons today as spiritual leaders in our churches, people who are just a notch above everybody else. In the first church it wasn't that way. Everybody was equal in the church, and these particular guys (there were seven of them at first) were appointed by the apostles to be the ones to make sure that everyone got enough to eat. They were servants within the church. They had a responsibility to meet a specific need of others. Their role was servant leadership.

A godly minister (which includes all Christians, for we are all called to be ministers) will not be afraid to get his hands dirty in the cause of the ministry. He should not be afraid to do menial tasks.

One of my professors at college said that, in rural churches in particular, a pastor has to learn to be a little of everything. Not only does he teach the Word from the pulpit, but he's got to be able and willing to sweep and mop the floors, clean the bathroom and do whatever it takes to keep that ministry going and be effective. The same thing is true when doing church-planting ministry. The leaders need to show a desire to "get down and get dirty" along with those they are hoping to minister to. People tend to be more willing to follow a fellow pilgrim than someone who doesn't understand their struggles.

If leaders don't have that kind of attitude, if people don't have that kind of humility, then they really need to reconsider their place in ministry, because they can become arrogant and proud. They may not mean to. They may not even recognize it when it happens. But pride and feelings of superiority can creep in and overtake anyone if he is not careful.

So Paul is a servant of Jesus Christ and in that he finds a delight and a joy. He is also called to be an apostle. He's called by God's grace (v. 5) and by God's choice. "We receive grace and apostleship." We, he says. I am not the only one. God chose us to be special ambassadors for Him. Paul realized his special calling, but he also acknowledged that he wasn't in this alone.

A godly pastor will recognize that his calling is greater than any secular vocation. Why is my ministry, or that of any other pastor, better than that of someone else like the telephone worker, the store clerk or the carpenter? Why is my job a little bit better? Only because the things that I am held responsible for as a pastor make an eternal difference. Buildings fall down. Communications systems break down or become outdated. Stores come and go. But people's lives are forever, and we need to invest in those. All things in this life are temporary except the soul in each one of us. Those are eternal. We, as pastors and teachers who are called to be representatives of God, are held responsible for the eternal state of people who sit under our ministry (Hebrews 13:17). That is not a light thing to be dealt with.

Bible teachers, at all levels, must also keep in mind that we are not alone in this endeavor to train people in godliness. In any active church ministry there is more than one capable and qualified (even gifted) teacher. Within any given community there are usually several, if not many, churches and parachurch ministries which have capable and godly leaders. We are definitely not alone in this calling. Those leaders who have come to the conclusion that their church, their leadership, or their teachings are the only correct ones have crossed the line from humble servant leaders to bold and arrogant declarers of agendas or doctrines that may or may not be biblically sound. Be aware, Christian, that you do not lift up your own thoughts above those of the Lord!

Our being set apart for the gospel of God is the second thing Paul talks about. Our primary role is to train and teach people how to live for God once they have discovered Him. It is my responsibility to be immersed in the Word of God, the Bible, so that every week when I teach it I can teach it accurately. I teach it as well as I possibly can through the power of the Holy Spirit. I pray that He will use my stumbling lips to aid some of you along the path of righteousness. It is my responsibility to teach each one of you from the Word of God how to live for God. That's not only on Sunday morning behind the pulpit, but that's in our daily or occasional meetings together, one-on-one or in small groups, continually nudging you or reminding you that we need to go back to the Bible for our answers. We need to check the Scriptures to know what direction to go, how to handle certain situations. That is my responsibility. That is what God has called a pastor to do. If I stick to that, I will always surrender my own thoughts and ideas to those presented in the Word for scrutiny, affirmation or correction.

So it is a preacher's delight to be a servant of God. It's also a preacher's delight to take advantage of opportunities to minister in and through expanded ministries as the Lord allows. They may take the form of a larger church, a more prominent role in current ministry, overseeing additional ministries within the local church or moving on to some other ministry altogether. It is not sinful to desire an expanded ministry as long as that desire is submitted to the will and leadership of the Lord Jesus.

The church at Rome had a reputation, Paul said (v. 8). "Your faith is being reported all over the world." Now Paul had not been to Rome yet. He had *hoped* to be there. It tells us he tried many times to go. For whatever reason, God didn't allow him to get to Rome. He said, "I still want to come and visit you guys. I've heard so much about you. Your faith is reported as being strong. Your faith has a reputation of being good. I wish I could go to Rome, visit you and say, 'I've been in that church and taught some of those people. I wish I could do that.'" He had hoped to do that soon. This letter that he wrote was intended to be a note to them declaring his intention to come and affirm his stand on the plan of salvation and how it fits into their relationship with each other, Gentile and Jew. So when he got there they would know where he stood and what he expected to teach. They would not be caught off guard.

Paul wanted to visit Rome because it was a well-established church. It was in the capitol of the world at that time, and it may have been one of the largest operating churches in his day because of the size of the city and the influence that they had.

Some people are not sure if it was majority Jewish or majority Gentile, because they don't know exactly how it was established. Quite probably, although there is not enough evidence to prove it, there were people from Rome at Jerusalem at the time of Pentecost, and they took the gospel back with them. Subsequently, home churches were established there at Rome. In that case, it would most likely have had a Jewish beginning. Others say Peter may have established it in his travels. We know he later became the head of the church at Rome. How it began does not really matter, because Paul addresses all people, Jew and Gentile alike, in this letter, and he would deal with both elements when he got there.

So we have his desire to be there. It would be like me wanting to go to some famous church of today. There aren't many that I really desire to be at. I could think of a couple that a lot of people would enjoy ministering in. One would be the Moody Church in Chicago that has a long-standing reputation of being a godly church, one that preaches the Word. A more modern one would be the Willow Creek ministry, which has also a good godly reputation. These two churches are totally different, and I don't know which I would fit into if I went. Neither one of them really appeals to me, and as I think about that I don't know that there is a particular church or ministry that I desire to be at and minister through just to say I've been there. However, if I were to say that there was a place I would like to go and teach the gospel in, I guess it would be the city of Jerusalem. I'd like to say I had a chance to visit Jerusalem and teach the gospel there, maybe once. I pray often for the nation of Israel and would like to visit it someday.

But for Paul, it was Rome. He wanted to go to Rome. He said he included that church in his prayers, is that maybe God will let him visit them.

Now we may look at that and say, isn't that being a little selfish? Paul wants to be there at that famous church to say he'd been there, so he prays to God to let him get there.

7

Perhaps, but I don't think so. Paul had a desire to teach the gospel wherever he was and wherever God allowed him to go, and I believe his prayer was that if God opened a way, as he says there in verse 10, he would go, but he would accept it also if he didn't go, as he had many times already. Wherever he was he would continue to teach and praise God for the church at Rome.

It should be a godly Christian's delight to proclaim the gospel to the world through whatever means God opens up to him. For Paul, we know God used many different avenues and many different locations. He did eventually end up in Rome, but not under the circumstances that he wanted. Teachers and pastors today should be ready and willing to teach the good news that Jesus saves and be faithful to it in our local congregations wherever they may be, but if God opens up an opportunity to go to Chicago, San Francisco, Washington D.C., Jerusalem, or any where else; we should not hold back if God clearly opens up the way. That may be an opportunity to meet and teach others that would never come a second time.

With today's technology we can reach the world without even leaving our homes or local churches. The need to travel has been greatly reduced, yet we can minister to large groups of people. The Internet has opened up a whole new means of reaching the world for Christ. Others have seized upon the opportunity to create easy access to all kinds of filth, degradation, and sinful behavior. Why should the servants of God be slow in capitalizing on such an open door? We should teach the good news however and wherever God opens it up for us.

This leads us to the third point. Paul says it should be

a Christian's delight to preach the gospel to whomever will listen. I'm obligated to both Greeks and non-Greeks, he says (v. 14), to both the wise and the foolish. In other words, I will speak to anybody who will listen.

The world then, as it is even today, was divided between Jews and non-Jews. If you're not Jewish you're Gentile, right? He says, I'd like to teach either one. It doesn't matter to me. I'm obligated to both the Greeks and the non-Greeks. If you're not Gentile, you're Jewish. If you are in the non-Jewish group (Greeks and barbarians, KJV), you're in the lower class group, at least from the Jewish perspective. We know that Paul was able to teach to those as well. He was understood by the wise as well as the foolish. He was able to do this because he was willing to talk to the people on their level, not allow his intelligence or education to interfere with his desire to share with them.

We should be ready to teach the gospel whenever the opportunity arises. It should be our desire to often and regularly teach the good news that Jesus saves. There should be no greater desire for any Christian than to do that. Why not? Why shouldn't there be other things that we might consider more important? What about going to a famous church? What about having a large congregation or a thriving ministry? What about teaching on love? What about this or that? No!

A godly Christian's primary and biggest desire should be to teach the gospel that Jesus saves (v. 16). "I'm not ashamed of the gospel, because it is the power of God for salvation to everyone who is willing to listen, to the Jew first and to the Gentile." I'm not ashamed to tell you that Jesus loves you, He died on the cross for you, and He rose again from the dead so you could have eternal life. I realize, as it says here, "it is the salvation of everyone who believes." That makes the difference between eternal hell and eternal salvation for you, if you put your faith in Jesus Christ. For it's in the gospel that righteousness comes and you receive a joy and a peace that can never be explained. It's through the gospel that lives are changed. People learn to live in love. People learn to live putting others first. People learn to be children of God; what it means to live by faith. Righteousness comes by faith. Paul says, "Just as it is written, 'the righteous will live by faith.'" These two verses are the theme of this whole book. He's going to go on and explain that in more detail as we go through.

As a pastor, my greatest delight is to continually, faithfully teach the gospel. If I ever lose that, God help me.

If you are a Christian reading this, then you should share this same compulsive desire. You should be taking advantage of every opportunity God gives you to share the good news that Jesus lives with everyone you meet. You and I are spokesmen for God to share the Gospel with anyone who will listen, wherever we may travel.

If you have never received Jesus into your life and realize for the first time that God is willing to accept you, just as you are, wherever you are; then go to Him and simply ask Him to receive you and take control. It doesn't matter if you're Jewish or Gentile. It doesn't matter what your race or nationality is. God's love knows no boundaries. Believe Him when he says, "He that cometh to me, I will in no wise cast out," (John 6:37, KJV).

CHAPTER 2

God's Answer to the Rationalist

Today's Bible Reading: Romans 1:18-32

> For since the creation of the world God's
> invisible qualities—his eternal power and
> divine nature—have been clearly seen,
> being understood from what has been
> made, so that men are without excuse.
> —Romans 1:20

It's really rather obvious as we look around us in the world that there's a lot of sin. Some of us think that as time goes on men get more and more degraded. With all the things that are available out there for people to be involved in, sin seems to be getting worse and worse. But is that really the case? Are we really any worse off now than at the time Paul wrote this letter in the first century?

If we look at this list of sins that he gives here (vv. 26-32), are they any different than what we see going on around us? Are there not people who are engaged in "shameful lusts" in our society? Are there not people who are full of every kind of wickedness, evil and depravity? All these things seem to be running rampant. Worship of many things other than the Creator God is common. We hear regularly about people being arrested for abusing children in many different forms. We hear of many, many different kinds of evil around us.

No, I don't think the world is any better or worse than it was. Men are still full of sin. Men are still sinful in their natural state, not because God made them that way but because of the sin of Adam and Eve at the time of the fall in the garden. From that time forward people have been choosing to sin and choosing to please themselves, rather than obey God.

People in our world today are in a very similar state to what Paul records here in the first century. If we look at the list of things that people were doing then, they are all things we know people are doing today. Children are disobedient to parents. People are senseless, that is they don't think carefully about the evidences all around us that point us back to the Creator. People are faithless and, yes, even ruthless in their dealings with each other in business. Crime is a constant problem wherever there are people. But the evidence is all around in our world today that God is real. God cares for those who participate in such things; God wants to save them. Yet, they choose to go their own way. Not only do they do that, but approve of people who do that as well. We see that in our society.

More and more we see that people encourage behaviors that would make our grandparents blush to even think about, let alone perform in public or talk about. Today there are public forums on all sorts of intimate or sexually explicit subjects. Participants discuss them as easily as today's weather. More often than not, there is either implicit or direct approval of the attitudes and behaviors involved even though there may be clear evidence that such behavior is self-destructive or clearly violates godly principles.

Even our court systems sometimes seem to approve of and are sympathetic toward certain sins by the rulings they make. More and more we are seeing judges make rulings that favor actions that are clearly contrary to the things God has declared to be right and holy. This becomes legal approval of sin. There is no other way to say it.

People are hopeless and helpless without God. There are many people in our world who have never heard of the grace of God because no one yet has told them.

Now, the Rationalist will tell you that because there is so much evil in our world and because there seems to be no intervention by a higher power, there probably is no such higher power, especially a God who cares. If there was a God who cared, they reason, He would put a stop to some or all of the pain, suffering and sin (so-called) around us.

The fact is, God repeatedly sent messengers to the people of the world, and at times He did use divine intervention to get their attention to show them that they were headed down the wrong path, but to no avail. There was a long string of prophets from the time of Abraham to Malachi. These were men God sent on the scene to point the world back to Himself. They were the judges, the kings, the prophets, or the rulers. Many of them were godly people who directed the Israelites and their neighbors back to God. For a time people would follow Him, then they would fall away again.

People ignore God, because they choose to serve their

own evil ways. They choose to do things the way they want to do them. They want to do things that feel good. They want to do things that seem natural. Yet the evidence is all around them that their way is wrong. "There is a way that seems right to a man, but in the end it leads to death," (Proverbs 14:15).

The Rationalist thought that God doesn't know or care about people is disproved by ancient history. As a part of His divine intervention to get people's attention in the world, He flooded the whole world at one point (Genesis 6-8). He destroyed everybody but one family. Did that work? Immediately after the flood there was sin and the cycle started all over again.

Later on, at the tower of Babel, He confused the languages of the people so they would scatter all over the world and not work together again to promote evil, worship false gods, and try to elevate themselves above God. Did that get their attention? No. They simply went their separate ways, developing many multiple and different cultures, and each one ignored God.

God destroyed Sodom and Gomorrah because the people of those towns refused to obey Him. They refused to live a godly lifestyle (Genesis 18-19).

Much later He allowed the nation of Israel to be destroyed and its people carried off into slavery in Babylon. This was a direct result of their disobedience to his commands and will for them. They had repeatedly refused to follow the path God had laid out for them, choosing instead to follow everybody else on a road of self-exaltation and false worship.

The list goes on, but the results have always been the same. Even though God has proven his supremacy and power, people still refuse to recognize or submit to Him. They prefer the easy routes of sin and selfishness. Ancient history shows us that God does care. He cared enough to deal with sin and degradation several times and in different ways. Each time He came to bring justified punishment on the ungodly or the disobedient. Every time He did that He also provided a means of escape. God always shows his mercy and forgiveness to those who are willing to accept it and turn from their wicked ways.

The Rationalist thought that God doesn't do anything about sin is also disproved by civil history. Every society and culture in the world has a system of moral standards. Some are more advanced than others. This moral code came from their roots in history. All nations originated from the tower of Babel. Before that they were all descendants of the family of Noah. That means that every tribe and ethnic group has the same foundation. The standards of accepted behavior is then, founded in Noah, who the Bible records, "found grace in the eyes of the Lord." So, all people groups have a foundation that is built on a relationship with God, although quite remote.

In each society, these standards are used to govern the people and punish offenders. This is referred to as civil rule. God uses civil rule to help keep sin in check. This has been true since people have organized themselves into communities. How successful it has been depends on your point of view. Nevertheless, God has not allowed sin to go unchecked in the world either by his direct intervention or by civil controls.

When evil rulers arise and abuse power at the expense of the lives of people, those nations who respect the dignity of life and abhor the atrocities of mass killing or ethnic cleansing will impose their influence to try to make it stop. Some times they are more successful than others. World War II is a classic example. The Nazi regime that led Germany during those terrible years of the '30s and '40s eventually were held accountable by those nations which recognized the value of human life and the right of every ethnic group to exist. There are basic civil "laws" that all nations and their leaders are held accountable for to some degree. It would be great if those "laws" were justly and fairly applied with some sense of regularity, but until Jesus comes that will not happen. But the point is that for a Rationalist to deny the evidence of civil controls as a deterrent to sin is to deny reality. And since all civil government is in place by the permission and will of God (Romans 13:1), God must then be using it to control sin, evil and the consequences of both.

The Rationalist thought that there is no evidence for God is disproved by natural history. There is enough evidence around us in nature to know there is a real, divine Creator. The existence of a deity is not found in the elements of creation. God is not in the tree. He's not the river. He's not a crocodile or the moose or the bear or anything else. He is greater than all those. His "eternal power and divine nature has been clearly seen," Paul says. When anyone focuses his mind on one object or a few objects within creation, he is embracing the messenger, not the One to whom the messenger points.

Within nature there is ample evidence of the Creator. Consider all the intricacies of a flower. Think about the minute details in the formation of various species of fish, shrimp, or some other life form. Everything is made in such a way that it fits *exactly* into its environment, and the ecosystem would be deficient without it. Consider the stars and their relationships to each other. Their number is beyond human comprehension, yet each one is important in the overall scheme of things. They influence our calendars and our climate. They are synchronized in such a way that their influences on each other form a balance and keep activity on a predictable course.

There is a recent rise in support for a theory labeled Intelligent Design. Basically, it says that science can no longer ignore the compelling evidence within nature that there had to be some form of higher intelligence to bring about the delicate and intricate elements that make up our world. Such evidence defies evolution at almost every turn. Evolution tries to ignore God as our Creator. Accurate scientific study of our world seems to say there has to have been one, based on the evidence.

Not only did God speak through the prophets, priests and kings. Not only did He interfere in history through divine intervention, but also He reveals Himself through creation. So people are without excuse. In spite of all that, most people still ignore Him or reject Him.

But God didn't leave it at that. He took one more opportunity to bring people back to Himself. He sent His Son to take upon Himself the sins of everyone in the world who would accept Him by faith.

The gospel, as presented in the New Testament through the coming of Christ, "is the power of God for salvation for everyone who believes" as Paul says in verse 16. That's what he is talking about in the rest of this chapter and the first part of chapter 2. Everyone who believes can be saved, including those who worship idols (v. 23), "They have exchanged the glory of the immortal God for things made to look like men, birds, animals, reptiles and other things in nature." Those people can be rescued. Those people can be saved once the salvation plan has been explained to them. Once they understand that God gave his only Son to save them, they don't need to worship nature or any of its elements any more.

Those who are involved in sexual immorality, in all its various forms can be saved. People tell us that homosexuality may be a genetic condition; may be an inherited condition. That's not what Scripture teaches. That's not the way God created men or women. People can be saved from that lifestyle into a more beneficial one. They can be brought into one that glorifies God; one that's more pleasing to God. There are many men and women who testify to that very truth, because they have been saved from that condition (see 1 Corinthians 6:9-11).

Those who intentionally teach false ideas about God, knowing the real truth, including the Rationalist who tries to explain God away, can be saved. Sometimes under the right conditions through the right person, God can confront them with their position. When they realize what they are doing is wrong and are convinced of their sin, they too can be saved.

I had a former pastor friend who taught in a local church for years before someone explained the plan of salvation to him. When he understood it he repented, got saved, and lived for God after that. He had been teaching false doctrine, but learned the truth, and the truth set him free.

In verse 25, Paul again talks about nature worship, not

only the elements of nature, but nature itself. "They exchange the truth of God for a lie, worship and serve created things rather than the Creator God."

Those involved in any form of evil activity (Paul's list is pretty lengthy here) may be saved. No matter what sin is in your life or mine, no matter what condition our neighbor or friends might find themselves in; we, and they, are not beyond hope. None of us are beyond help, because God is more powerful than any sin that we might be involved in. God is more powerful than any evil that anybody may be practicing.

In the Gospel of John, Jesus Himself said people in the world often would rather perform their evil deeds than come under the scrutiny of the light of the gospel because that's going to reveal their deeds for what they are (John 3:19,20). They're going to be exposed to the world. But every man since Adam, every woman since Eve has been under the curse of sin, and that sin brings judgment of God. That sin is subject to punishment unless it is forgiven; unless it's cleansed under the blood of Christ.

Those who may be involved in any activity known to man, any form of evil or sin, including Rationalism, can be rescued if they simply put their faith in Christ, trust Him for their salvation, give Him their lives, and exercise faith that He will give them hope and joy. No one is beyond hope. No one is outside the reaches of the Spirit of God.

Let's remember that truth when we're talking to our coworkers. Let's remember that truth when we think of the people whose names are in the newspaper and on the television or radio news for their great sins and their crimes. Those people are not beyond the reach of God. Let's pray for them. Let's support the ministries that are trying to reach them. If we know people who are without Christ, let's reach out to them. Let's share the gospel with them. Jesus loves them, and Jesus wants them to be saved.

"For the power of God is the salvation of everyone who believes."

CHAPTER 3

God's Answer to the Moralist

Today's Bible Reading: Romans 2:1-16

For it is not those who hear the law who are
righteous in God's sight, but it is those who
obey the law who will be declared righteous.
(Indeed, when Gentiles, who do not have
the law, do by nature things required by
the law, they are a law for themselves, even
though they do not have the law, since they
show that the requirements of the law are
written on their hearts, their consciences
also bearing witness, and their thoughts
now accusing, now even defending them).
—Romans 2:13-15

All of us are aware of the tragedies that have struck the
Kennedy family. That whole family has had a history
of tragedy as you probably know. When President John
Kennedy was assassinated, when Robert Kennedy was
killed, what did you hear through the media about these

two men? Praise. Good things. They were good men. They were leaders in our country. They were people we could look up to.

Perhaps people you know have passed away. At their funeral or when talking to their friends and relatives, someone will say, "He (or she) was a good person, and I'm sure God has blessed him and received him (or her)."

Well, this whole passage is God's answer to those people who say, "My life and my action will count for good. I try to be good in all that I do, therefore God will accept me."

The Moralist is a person who says, "I'm not as bad as other people. There is always someone else worse than I am. I don't do some of the things that other people do. The activities of some people are much worse than my own. I don't cheat. I don't kill. I don't steal. I don't commit rape. The people who do those things are condemned. They're evil. I'm not like that. God's going to accept me because I'm not like that."

In Luke (18:9-14), Jesus told the story of one man who stood up in worship and said, "God, look at me. I'm glad I'm not like that guy. I'm good. I come to worship every week. I fast. I pray and give generously to the work of God. Isn't that enough?"

What was Jesus's answer? The one who fell on his face and said, "God, I'm not worth it. I'm nothing in front of you, but thank you for loving me," that man is justified.

The Moralist will say, "I'm good because I'm not evil. Therefore, I must be accepted by God." God's response is that everyone is a sinner in need of a Savior. No exceptions. We often quote Paul from the third chapter of this very book where he says, "For all have sinned and fall short of the glory of God."

We can look back, all the way back to Genesis, and see that this theme has been in existence from the beginning. The earliest record of this statement being made, even though the truth was evident before it, was in the book of Job. Job was a contemporary of Abraham, early on in history. Job mentions (4:17) the fact that there is no one alive that does not sin.

Everyone is a sinner in need of a Savior. The Moralist doesn't recognize that. He says, "I'm good, therefore God will accept me." He also thinks that God will accept him, not in comparison to somebody else, but based on the good things he has done. He says, "I'm not bad. I don't do the things that those terrible people do. I do things that are good. That should be why God will accept me."

Paul wrote (v. 6), God would judge and punish or reward each person according to what he has done. He was quoting another place from back in the Old Testament (Psalm 62:12). The Moralist will say, "That's my key. That's the verse I'm going to claim. I'll take that and v. 7 with it as my key statement. If I do good works and persistently try to do well, God is going to accept me and give me eternal life.

Actually, that statement in v. 6 *is* correct. God *will* give to each person according to what he has done. To the unsaved people that is true only to the point of what they have done with their knowledge of God, as we saw back in chapter one. They know by looking around that God exists. If they worship Him to the extent of their knowledge of Him, fine. If they reject the evidence for God and go their own way and worship false gods, doing all kinds of evil as is mentioned there, then they will be punished for that. They will receive just what their lifestyle deserves— destruction. The person who has never heard God's simple plan of salvation as revealed in the New Testament, will still have no excuse. God's evidence is still all around us. So, yes, it is true that a person will be judged according to what he has done with the information about God that he has.

Now, if they have accepted Christ because they have heard the plan of salvation in its fullness, good deeds are the basis of their judgment. Such a person has acted in response to the good news of Jesus's sacrificial death and forgiveness. That action as well as all others done for and in the name of Christ afterward is the basis of His judgment.

Just as there is ample evidence of the Creator in our world, the basic elements of God's plan of salvation are evident in the world around us as well. Think about it. It's common knowledge that everybody sins, right? Even though some try to deny it, they know it's true. They know they have lied at some point. They know they have disobeyed their parents somewhere along the line. Everybody knows that everybody sins. You can probably think of some sins in your own life without trying too hard. That is the first element of the plan of salvation. You must recognize that you are a sinner.

Everybody knows that when there is a breakdown in a relationship there needs to be reconciliation before the relationship can be healed and restored. In order to be reconciled to the one you have offended you have to go to that person and confess the wrong and make it right. That's confession of sin, another basic element of the plan of salvation.

Thirdly, if you want to make it right with God, it takes faith. Just as it takes faith to believe the one you have offended will even listen to you to begin the healing process, it takes faith to believe that God exists and that God is willing to listen to you and forgive you (Hebrews 11:6).

Those are the three basic elements of the plan of salvation. You must recognize you are a sinner, you must confess your sin, and then you must accept by faith that God will forgive you, specifically, through the power of Jesus Christ. Even if you don't know about Him, the elements are still true.

So the Moralist really has no excuse. It's true that everybody will be judged according to what they have done, but is it what they have done with their knowledge of Christ or what they have done after receiving Christ?

The Moralist denies the concept that all sins are equal in the sight of God. Little sins God overlooks. Big sins He hates. That's not what Scripture teaches. If you have sinned, you have sinned. You go hunting and shoot at a deer. If you hit the tree next to it or the ground in front of you, it makes no difference. The deer is still going to run away. You can't fill your freezer if you can't hit the target. You can't miss by an inch and claim victory. The concept of all sins being equal is what the Moralist denies.

In fact, he has developed a sense of pride in his own accomplishments. What is pride? It's a sin. "I'm good. I have succeeded. I have accomplished many things. I have given half my inheritance to charity. I work for nonprofit organizations to help my neighbor. I do all kinds of things." God's answer: That's all well and good, but you're not perfect. Everyone is a sinner no matter how small the infraction.

25

God looks down on man and says, "Is there a righteous man down there anywhere? No. Not even one," (Psalm 53:1, 3). There's no one righteous outside the power of God. We're all evil and prone to do evil. When a Moralist claims to be good, he is actually lying to himself (and everyone else), which nullifies his claim to goodness. He is as much a sinner as everyone else.

A Moralist will also try to use his conscience as his guide, Paul says in these last few verses. That means he acts in accordance to the way he feels. "If my conscience doesn't bother me when I'm doing something, then it must be okay. It must be all right. If I don't feel guilty about punching my neighbor or shooting his dog or whatever it might be, it's got to be okay because my conscience says it's all right."

We have seen and felt the consequences of that kind of teaching in our world. If it feels good do it. We've seen the desecration. The person with that attitude acts in a manner that is most pleasing to himself rather than anybody else. He says, "If I feel good about this, if it pleases me, if it makes me feel good, then I'm going to do it. If it makes me feel a little closer to God, I'm going to do it." He's self-centered. God's answer, Paul says, to this kind of thinking is that you cannot trust your conscience. God puts it in you as a measuring guide and to act as a protection for your own good, but you can't trust it. I'll tell you why.

How many times have you felt a prick in your conscience about something you were tempted to do and you went ahead and did it anyway? Your conscience can be overruled by your mind. If your mind is not submitted to the mind of Christ, you're going to overrule your conscience at times to do what you want to do which means your conscience is not your supreme power or influence. So you shouldn't use it as your guide.

In fact, Paul says in these verses that God's going to use your conscience against you at the judgment. If your conscience has said, don't go into that place or don't go to that particular event and you went anyway; you've overruled your conscience. You're going to be held accountable for that, because God gave you your conscience so you wouldn't do that and you did it anyway.

And then he says God's going to judge people on their awareness of Him, disregarding their conscience. Yes, the conscience is going to be a part of his judgment. He's going to use that, but going back, again, to the original thought, it doesn't matter if your conscience bothers you or not. You're still going to be judged on your awareness of God, your relationship with God. Your thoughts, he says, sometimes accuse you, and sometimes defend you. You can't trust your thoughts. You can't trust your conscience; all you've got left is your relationship with God. What is that like?

Those who disregard God and his evidence are going to be condemned. Again we go back to what Jesus said in John 3:36, "Everyone who believes in the Son will be saved, but those who reject him are already still under the condemnation of God." Those who submit to God's leadership, his kingship, his rule, will be given their reward.

Now, lastly, we see God's judgment of the Moralist will occur at the final judgment (v. 16). "God will judge men's secrets through Christ," it says. There is a long list of passages that reveal this to us. We can look at Revelation 20, Malachi 3, Luke 10, and others that tell us that there will be a judgment day. There will come a final day when all our secrets will be judged according to what we have done with our lives and our ministries after we have received Christ.

The list in God's Book of Life will be His sole criteria for admission into eternal glory with Him. If your name is there, and it can be, you're guaranteed a place. In Revelation chapter 20, it says, "Those whose names are written in the Book of Life will receive eternal glory." Now what is this book of life? What is it like? How can we get our names there?

Well, as I did some research through Scripture, I discovered that most Bible teachers, and myself, up to recently, had everything backwards. I always thought that your name was written there the day you accepted Christ as your Savior. But that's not what I found. Let's go back to the early teachings on this subject and work through. You will find that people's names are already in the Book of Life, but at some point they are *wiped out*. At some point in everybody's life they may or may not have their name *erased* from the book. (By the way, this backs up the theory of innocence for children. When you are born you are born under the love and grace of God, and if you die before the age of accountability, you are taken into His presence).

Three things were listed specifically that would cause God to erase a person's name. One is flagrant sin. If you do something against God and His work, your name is wiped out because you have rejected God and actually worked in opposition to God. (Exodus 32:31-34, Psalm 69:28) People like the atheistic activist, the champion of Christian haters, or a national leader who forces believers to deny God or be punished, expelled or killed would have their names wiped out.

Another is for rejecting Christ once you have heard the gospel. If you say no, that's not for me; I'd rather go my own way, live my own life, and take my chances, then your name is wiped out. You are what the Bible calls an apostate. You have been given one or more chances to make things right between yourself and God and choose not to. Why should God not wipe our name off the list? If you reject Him, why should He not reject you? (Malachi 3:16-18)

The third reason is for ignoring God through this life. You have just not paid any attention to the Christians using all the media at their disposal to try to relate the love of God and knowledge of God. If you ignore all that, thinking it was not for you, your name is wiped out when you die (Hebrews 12:22-25). Notice the patience of God. He will give you your entire life to turn to Him for forgiveness and reconciliation, but once you leave this world your destiny is sealed. If you have not taken that step of faith and allowed Him to take control, your name is erased forever from the Book of Life.

So there are two groups of people left, those who have received Christ and little babies. When we stand before the judgment seat of God and He opens the Book, He's only going to see the names of little babies and everyone who has accepted Him by faith (Revelation 3:5, 21:27). Then He'll say, "Come in. Welcome to my home."

The Moralist's name can be in that book if he chooses to accept Christ and let Him be in control. The Moralist who says, "I am good and God will accept me," should be in that book if he changes that to say, "I'm not good. God, please accept me. Please forgive me. All the good things I do from now on will be to Your honor and glory not mine."

There is hope for the Rationalist (chapter 1) and for the Moralist here in the first part of chapter 2. There is hope for anyone because as long as you're alive, God is willing to receive you. If you just simply and humbly come to Him and ask forgiveness. Keep in mind, we cannot be saved by how good we are or by the works we have accomplished. We can only be sure of having our names in the Lamb's Book of Life if we come to Him by faith and declare our sinfulness and let Him cleanse us and forgive us. "For it is by grace you have been saved, through faith—and this not from yourselves, it is the gift of God—not by works, so that no one can boast. For we are God's workmanship, created in Christ Jesus to do good works, which God prepared in advance for us to do," (Ephesians 2:8-10).

CHAPTER 4

God's Answer to the Legalist

Today's Bible Reading: Romans 2:17-3:4

> A man is not a Jew if he is only one
> outwardly, nor is circumcision merely
> outward and physical. No, a man is a Jew
> if he is one inwardly, and circumcision is
> circumcision of the heart, by the Spirit,
> not by the written code. Such a man's
> praise is not from men, but from God.
> —Romans 2:28, 29

I want to start this lesson by taking a glimpse at two kinds of churches.

At the first church you walk in and all the men are dressed in coats and ties with brightly polished shoes. They walk around like they've got a rod up their backs. The women are dressed in fancy dresses and hats. Some of them have white gloves on. Every part of the service, as you sit through it, seems to be scripted. Everybody knows exactly what's going on, when it's going to happen, and how long it will take. When the preacher preaches, he deals heavily with Christian behavior and the need to follow strict teaching of that church. There is a strong sense of ritual and formality. You wonder how much of this service really impacts the lives of those who participate.

You go to another church the next week. In that church you find everyone is dressed alike in plain simple clothes. No fancy clothes or jewelry. The men sit on one side of the room, the women and children on the other. There's no discernible order to the service. People just start singing when they feel like it or praying as they are led. But the main speaker of the morning emphasizes that piety comes from shunning all selfish pleasure, which they see as sin. It's foolish to laugh and joke and have fun, especially on Sunday.

It appears these two types of churches have fallen into the same trap that orthodox Jews of history have fallen into. That is, the trap of legalism. They appear to be more concerned about adherence to the rules and regulations as they understand them and promote them than they are to God.

A strict Legalist sometimes will brag about how well he keeps the rules and laws. I've even met some people who say, "We have a fixed way of doing things in our congregation. We know what is expected of everybody within our congregation and I think I'm doing pretty well keeping those rules."

What does Paul say on that subject to the church at Rome? What is God's answer to the Legalist; that person who is bound up by rules and regulations? Well, the first thing he says in verses 17-24, is that legalists condemn themselves because they can't even keep the laws that are on the books or that they put on the books. They fail to live up to the law.

If it's not a hundred percent, it's not enough. Because if you break one, as we're told about the laws of the Old Testament, you've broken them all. You're just as much a sinner as anybody else.

We go back to Matthew 19:16-22, Jesus is talking to a young man there. The young man asked Jesus, "What shall I do to inherit eternal life?"

Jesus says, "Obey the rules. Keep the commandments."

He says, "I've done that from the time I was young. I've kept all the rules." Jesus knew better and the young man knew better, too.

Then Jesus said, "All right, there's one more thing I want you to do. I want you to step outside the rules for a minute. Sell everything you own and give it away."

"I can't do that," was the answer. That was a requirement he refused to obey. By disobeying what Jesus asked of him he broke all the rest. His pride amounted to nothing.

People who are bound up in Legalism cannot keep the rules. They are too binding and rigid. They end up breaking them, and they're no better off than those who didn't keep them. They are proven to be failures.

What's more, Paul says in verse 24, the result is that people outside the church of Rome or any legalist group see that failure as a good reason to stay away. People despise and disregard the god that sets people up for a fall. Would you like to be involved in a system where you could not meet the criteria? Every week as you assemble, it is pointed out to you that you have not succeeded? What kind of mental attitude would you gain after a while? You would be proven or shown that you can't do it, and you would wonder if there is any hope.

Do legalists offer hope, really? I wonder if they do. If their god lets them down because they break the rules, it's not a god of love, compassion or grace. Where is forgiveness? Where is faith? A legalist fails to live up to the law that he has chained himself to. Paul goes on to say that submission to God is better than submission to a law—any legal system, whether it be from the Old Testament commandments or particular ritual that was performed by the Jews. He uses circumcision as an example of what they are doing to prove his point. The Jews went through this ritual of male circumcision that represented their adherence to God through keeping the Law. But Paul says those who are circumcised physically tried to keep the Law and failed. They didn't get anywhere. But those outside of the Law, the Gentiles, the ones who were not circumcised, believed in God and they keep the principles of the commandments.

You remember what Jesus said the two principles of the commandments are? It boils down to two things: Love the Lord your God with all your heart and love your neighbor as yourself. If you do that, even if you don't keep the Law, you are right with God (Matthew 22:37-40). So, those who are circumcised, if they fail to keep the law are no better off than people who didn't even have the Law in the first place. Anyone who kept those two principles were blessed by God and accepted by him.

The Law is impossible to keep in its entirety. We've seen that by example. We can see that in the lives of some people we know as well. You and I are no better off than those who never attempted to keep it. In fact, in Jeremiah 9, God says there is a punishment going to come to all those who attempt to live under the Law and fail. Now where does that leave you and me? Not in a very good position.

Obedience to God should come from the heart. As Paul calls it here in verse 29, "circumcision of the heart by the Spirit, not by the written code." In other words, we don't need to go through any ceremonial ritual to make ourselves right with God. All we need to do is submit to the leadership of the Holy Spirit. All we need is to follow the Scriptures as they are written and submit when we see something in Scripture that points out to us that we have been wrong, and then we confess that and change it. However, let's not become so strict that we put ourselves in chains. Let the Spirit guide us. Let the Spirit direct us. Let Him convict us and change us on a daily basis.

This whole idea of the Law as a chain or a system that has bound people with no chance of escape is one that many people can't or don't recognize. They either don't know any better or they are so used to all the rules and regulations that they don't know any other way to worship or live. Some do not see the structure of church life as being binding or enslaving. Others would not know how to live outside the regulations given to them by others.

I maintain that obedience from the heart, led by the Spirit is the way we should go. Go to Hebrews 11, that famous faith chapter, and read down through the list of names recorded there. God, according to their faith, accepted the first ten individuals or groups of people mentioned. All of them lived and operated before the Law was even established. That tells me that the Law had a different purpose. It never was intended to save them or offer them deliverance from sin. It was never intended to be a substitute for faith. It was intended, instead, to be a guideline for life. A life lived by faith. Faith has always been the basis on which God has accepted people.

So, where does that leave us? Do we throw out the Law and live exclusively by faith and the leading of the Holy Spirit? When we come to worship on Sunday morning do we all just come to church, quiet ourselves in the seats and then just wait for things to happen? No. That's not what Paul says.

We don't throw the Law away just because it is sometimes misused. Chapter three, verse one asks, "What advantage is there in being a Jew?" Today we might ask a strict Legalist, Is there any value in legalism or in the rites within services? Yes. There is some value in them if these churches are indeed Christian churches, because they, along with all the others, have the very words of God. They are teaching Scripture.

In another place Paul tells us that some people were working against him. They were challenging him; they were trying to ridicule and put down Paul and at the same time promote themselves and their ministries. Paul says, "I don't care. Let them do that as long as they proclaim the Word of God. I don't care if they put me down as long as the gospel is bring preached," (Philippians 1:15-18).

So we see that we should not condemn legalistic churches as long as they're teaching the Word of God. As long as they are teaching people that the Bible says salvation is through Christ, not their system of laws. If they are doing that, then we should not judge them or condemn them. So what if some people who live under the Law (or church regulations) fail to keep it? What difference does it make to me? It doesn't nullify the Law. It only shows that the rules are being misused. They should be guides to draw us closer to God, not as a means of redemption. They should point us to the Savior, not be a means of our salvation.

Neither does it nullify God's faithfulness. That's the most important note here. Just because some people fail doesn't mean God fails. Remember God is not human. God is Spirit. He *was* human in the form of Christ for a period of thirty years or so, and he retained that physical nature in a new and unique form after the resurrection. But God is not limited to humanity, and God's faithfulness far supersedes any of our own. We fail. Some of us fail often. God does not.

Instead of people being chained to the legalistic way of life, may they instead be living under the leadership of the Holy Spirit. We should want to live for God. We should want to put God first in our lives. When God speaks to me and judges me of my sin, I will accept that judgment. Not because the Law says I'm wrong, but because the Spirit prompts me and asks me to change.

What is God's answer to the Legalist, then? Set yourself free from the Law. Instead of obeying the Law, obey Me. Instead of being so bound up with rules and regulations let the Spirit direct you in the way you should live. Substitute your legalistic lifestyle for a life of faith. That's something we all need to be careful of. Be watchful. Be watchful over your life, and I will over mine, that we might live to the glory of God, not under the Law.

CHAPTER 5

God's Answer to the Skeptic

Today's Bible Reading: Romans 3:3-8

> What if some did not have faith?
> Will their lack of faith nullify
> God's faithfulness? Not at all!
> —Romans 3:3,4a

There are some people that can find a negative aspect to anything. I read an article in a newspaper about a lady who was so negative that her own family couldn't stand her any more. Everything that came up in a conversation she would make out to be a bad thing or have a negative thought to express about it. She was one of those people who always look on the bad side of any situation. Perhaps you know someone like that.

So far we have looked at three different types of people: the Rationalist, the Moralist and the Legalist. Now Paul is going to address the Skeptic. The skeptic is the one who looks at things and says, "What's the use?" He has a negative attitude about everything.

Let's look at what it says in chapter three and read verses 3-8.

> What if some did not have faith? Will their lack of faith nullify God's faithfulness? Not at all! Let God be true, and every man a liar. As it is written: "So that you may be proved right when you speak and prevail when you judge."
>
> But if our righteousness brings out God's righteousness more clearly, what shall we say? That God is unjust in bringing his wrath on us (I am using a human argument.) Certainly not! If that were so, how could God judge the world? Someone might argue, "If my falsehood enhances God's truthfulness and so increases his glory, why am I still condemned as a sinner?" Why not say—as we are being slanderously reported as saying and as some claim that we say—"Let us do evil that good may result?" Their condemnation is deserved.

There are two major questions here that a Skeptic will ask. Let's look at the first one. This question is asked in a variety of ways: "There are people who claim to be Christians who don't live up to the truth of Scripture, so why even try? There are people in churches every Sunday who go out from worship and don't even speak the name of Jesus at all during week. They live like they don't believe anything that is taught in church, so why should I believe?" Or "Some people fail God. If someone has a lack of faith, why should I try to have faith? What's the point? If God doesn't honor their faith, why should I exercise faith? Isn't God going to fail me, too?"

People who go to church and claim to be Christians are subject to sin and a lack of faith. Do we all have perfect faith? Do you have perfect faith? Everything you want within the will of God, does it happen? Do we have the kind of faith that Jesus says we can have to say to this mountain, "Remove yourself into the sea," and it happens. Do we have the kind of faith to say, "Lord, fix our church audio equipment so it doesn't mess up in the middle of a service?" If we had that kind of faith and it worked, wouldn't it strengthen our resolve? Wouldn't it strengthen our faith and encourage it to grow? Perhaps. But the fact is, all of us don't have strong faith. Some of us are weak in our faith.

Faith grows through exercise. If we have a little bit and use it, and God answers, we're going to say, "Yes, I can trust God. He hears me. So I'll do it again." Faith grows by using it just like muscles in our bodies. If we don't use our muscles they're not going to grow. They're not going to be limber or strong. In fact, the medical experts tell us that if you don't use a limb for a long time it's going to get stiff. The muscles will actually deteriorate, and you'll lose them. That's why they'll tell you after an operation to exercise, to loosen up, and to strengthen your muscles. You'll lose it if you don't use it.

My mother used to say that about her children's intelligence. She said, "God gave you a brain. Use it or you're going to lose it." Well, I think I may have lost a few parts over the years. I'm not sure I exercise my brain as much as I should. But that's a whole other matter.

Faith grows through exercise. We need to exercise our

faith and keep on expecting answers. Then we will know that God really does hear us.

Sometimes when we exercise our faith, we don't see the answers we expect. Why not? James tells us if you ask and you don't really believe you're going get the answer, you're not going to get the answer. If you ask with a doubt in your mind, you might as well not ask (James 1:6, 7).

That's not faith. Faith says, "God I need a new car, because mine is broken down, there's nothing I can do about it. I'm trusting you, and I'm going to go to work tomorrow in a replacement vehicle." That's faith.

Faith says, "VBS is going to start tomorrow morning. I expect the workers are going to teach about fifty children, and I'm going to try to get those fifty. My faith says there will be fifty kids here before the week is over." Faith asks for those things that you realistically cannot bring about on your own. What does Hebrews 11:1 say? "Faith is the substance of things not yet seen, the hope of things to come."

Faith says, "I know it's going to happen through the power of God." That means faith relies on something outside of ourselves. We cannot rely on ourselves or someone else to deliver the answer to our dilemma. It has to depend on a higher power, which is God himself.

So, what if some people's faith is weak or is not visible or evident? Does that mean that God is not faithful? No. God's faithfulness does not depend on the strength of your faith or mine. God is God. He is true in all aspects, and his character does not change. It is not dependent on us. It does not change at all just because of our strength or weakness. God is who He is in spite of our weakness. If God's character fluctuated, changed, and adjusted itself according to our faith, how could we trust him? What kind of strength would he have? He would be a very weak God, because we, in fact, would control him instead of He us. God's character does not depend on our faith or us. Our faith is weak or strong as the time and circumstances require it. God is constant and sure. He "does not change like shifting shadows," (James 1:17).

So, to answer the question: "If there are some people in church who have weak faith, why should I trust God?" God can be trusted no matter how the people act. God's strength, God's power, does not depend on the people. He is separate and independent of people. He is also very much superior to people.

The second question the Skeptic will ask is: "Well, if God's grace, God's faithfulness, God's mercy is evident by His forgiveness of sin, wouldn't it be better if I sinned on purpose so God's grace would be even more evident to the unbelievers?"(vv. 5-8).

That may sound like a ridiculous question. But, when you think about it, from an unbeliever's viewpoint that might be a logical question. If God's grace is evident through His forgiveness of someone's sin, why can't they sin regularly and go back regularly for forgiveness? Isn't this, in fact what some churches teach? Each week or every time you have an opportunity you can go into the church or to the church leaders and ask forgiveness and go from there and do as you please, knowing that you can come back and ask forgiveness again. Doesn't that show that God is a God of grace and love and forgiveness?

Well, let's let Scripture answer the question. First of all, sin must be judged no matter what the motive is. If my motive is selfishness, greed or anything else and I honestly confess that and ask for forgiveness, God's going to forgive that even though there may be consequences. That sin still has to be dealt with and judged. If my motive is to try to make God look good by being bad, that doesn't matter. Sin is sin. God will deal with that. No matter what the motive is, sin has to be dealt with.

Now if a person does it regularly and intentionally, we must ask ourselves if the repentance and the confession are real. The Scriptural answer is no. It is not. If you recognize a sin in your life, whatever it might be; greed, selfishness, a sexual sin, a moral sin; and you go to God for forgiveness, but two days later you find yourself doing it again, knowing it is wrong; you didn't really mean it the first time. If you find yourself repeating that sin several times, those confessions are not real. Face it. If you truly repented, if you truly asked God for help, you wouldn't want to do it again, because you would be offending the all-powerful, almighty God, knowing that His judgment would come down on you for that. A repeated sin is not a repented sin. So, if you do this particular sin, trying to make God look good, it's not going to work, because your sins are not forgiven in those situations.

On the other hand, if you are faithful to Him and you truly confess a sin, get it out of your life and move on, trying to live faithfully for God; his grace, mercy, and love are not going to be diminished.

If you poke a hole in a balloon, how much of the air comes out? Can you get just a little bit of air out of a balloon? No. It's the same way with God's love and God's mercy. When you commit a sin and you admit it, asking God's forgiveness, the fullness, the completeness of God's grace and love, is poured out to you for that forgiveness and cleansing, not just a little bit. So you don't need to try to increase God's love. You don't need to try to increase His forgiveness, because you can't. You've already got it all. There is no more. When you have the fullness of God in your life, you have the power of God to overcome sin. You have the power of the Holy Spirit within you to resist sin (1 Cor. 10:13). You have everything you need. You cannot increase it by intentionally repeating a sin.

God's love, his power, and his grace were intended for and will continue to be poured out for the forgiveness of the repentant sinner, whether it be for salvation or for the confession of sin, and will always be that way because God's nature doesn't change.

God's love will continue to be applied to each one of us when we face sin in its fullness and we recognize its evil intent. When we recognize that it does not sit well with God and we ask truly in faith, believing that God will forgive us, he will—fully and completely.

Should we say, "Let's do evil that good may result?" Paul says no. If you think that way, you're going to be condemned in your sins, because you're continually sinning. You are offending the true nature of God. Remember, it is the intent of your heart that God is judging more than the deeds themselves. If you don't intend to give up the sins you confess, he knows it and withholds his forgiveness.

So, how should we answer a Skeptic; that person who says, "Why should I believe in God if I see other people's faith fail?" We answer by shifting his focus from the people to God. People fail. God is faithful. You can trust God because God can be trusted. He is God, not a man. God is good no matter what. God is gracious, no matter what. God wants to pour out His love, His power, His Spirit on you, no matter what you've done.

If you've not received the power of God in your life, if you want to be forgiven of any sin in your life completely— to get it out, get it done with—go to God in prayer. Confess it honestly and ask the Spirit to guide you to be free. Then, as Jesus often said, go and sin no more.

The Skeptic is truly not a Christian. He doesn't trust God. Do you? Have you come to Jesus for the saving power? Do you have the Holy Spirit living in you empowering you, loving you? I pray that you have. If not, I pray that you will do that right now.

CHAPTER 6

No Exceptions

Today's Bible Reading: Romans 3:9-20

What shall we conclude then? Are
we any better? Not at all! We have
already made the charge that Jews and
Gentiles alike are all under sin.
—Romans 3:9

Suppose you went to a car dealer to buy a new car. Yours is getting worn out, and you decide you need to get another one. You go down to the local dealership, you walk around the lot, and you see all kinds of different autos. Of course you're not there more than two or three minutes before a salesman's right there at your elbow.

"How can I help you? What can I do for you?"

You say, "Well, I kind of like this vehicle right over here."

He replies, "That's a good one. You've made a good choice."

"Well, what does it have for options or accessories?"

He lists off all the different things and includes in the list four radial tires.

You say, "What? Four tires? Doesn't every car come with four tires?"

Normally we would expect so, but apparently, according to an ad seen in a flyer recently, certain dealers consider them as options. Every car needs tires to go off the lot. You shouldn't expect to pay extra for them. It would be foolish to buy a car and have to buy tires before you could leave the garage.

Just as people expect cars to have certain things that are actually options (which vary according to make and model) they expect things from God sometimes that God does not provide. Wanting options on your car may not be unreasonable, but sometimes people expect things from God that are unreasonable. They may come to God and say, "I expect you to accept me as I am without change. I offer no options."

That's not what the Scripture says should be happening. The Bible says you should come to God and expect change in your life and the lives of people around you.

We've already said that Paul talked about four different types of people up to this point in his letter and with each one he dispels their argument of how they can approach God and expect to be received (Lessons 2-4).

Now Paul is in a summary mode, and he asks, "What shall we conclude, then? Looking at ourselves, are we any better than any of these four types of people; the Moralist, the Legalist, the Rationalist, or the Skeptic; with which we may not identify ourselves? Are we any better off than they?

No." Even if we don't fit neatly into one of these four boxes we're no better off. The reason is that we've already made the charge that Jews and Gentiles, which means everybody, are under sin. Every single person who has ever lived has sinned. So, where does that leave us? Where does that leave you in your relationship with God? You're no better or worse than the next guy. You're no different from anybody else. You are a sinner like the rest of us.

The Jewish people thought they had a special sense or special right to a relationship with God simply because they were descendants of Israel. Not so. They are set apart as a nationality, as an ethnic group, to be a special people for God, as a remnant for God to work through. But as individuals, Jewish people need a Savior just as much as Gentiles do. They have no special options there.

For those of us who grew up in a Christian church where we heard the plan of salvation taught regularly, where the church was good in relating the Scriptures and in trying to get the people to live by the Scriptures, are we any better off? If anyone has never taken that step of faith for salvation, he is still lost in his sins. There is no difference. There is no one who is exempt from sin. We all are subject to it.

Paul quotes six passages from the Old Testament to prove his point.

First, he makes a general statement, quoting from Psalm 53, which is also a quote from Psalm 14. The words are identical in those two Psalms where David reminds us that there is no one on earth anywhere who is good enough for God, good enough to stand in the presence of God, or good enough to be accepted by God. All of us, Paul reminds us there in verse 12, at some point have turned away from God and gone our own way.

We all know that to be true, don't we? We know there have been times in our own lives when we knew what God wanted from us, but we say, "I'd rather do this instead. I would rather be doing something else than what You asked me to do."

My motive for going to bible college was different from what God's plan was. I went to bible college with the intention of becoming a Christian schoolteacher. People told me, even before I left, I should probably consider the ministry, but I didn't want that. My desire was a classroom with children up to fourteen years old. God said, through circumstances, through time, "I want you in the ministry." That's where He directed me.

I could have refused. I could have been stubborn. I could have gone my own way and waited out an opportunity to serve in a Christian school. Looking back on it now, I think probably I would have been unhappy because I would not be doing God's will. I would be doing my will, even though it's God's work.

People need to understand that all of us go our own way at times. Even within ministries and even with the best of intentions it's still a sin. So, none of us are exempt from sin.

Then Paul talks about some practical or more precise ways people sin. One is with the way they speak. "Their throats are open graves, their tongues practice deceit and their lips spit out poison," to rephrase what he says in verse 13.

People talk in cynical ways. The Apostle James knew that well, didn't he? He spent a whole chapter in his letter discussing the control of the tongue. His conclusion was that it is just about impossible for us to do that without the help of the Holy Spirit. People tend to wag their tongues in negative ways. It's easy to say something negative about somebody else. It's easy to put someone else down. It's a natural tendency and we have to be careful. That is one way people commit sin.

According to verses 15 and 16, "People are swift to shed blood, ruin and misery mark their ways." Now not all of us (in fact, I hope very few people compared to the total population) are ready and willing to shed blood, to kill one another or to injure people seriously. Yet, how many people in our society don't think twice about taking advantage of someone else, ruining somebody else to make themselves look good or to improve their business. They do things that are jeopardizing other people's lives to promote themselves or their industries. God says ruin and misery mark their ways. They will bring other people to ruin and misery to promote and elevate themselves. In the long run the tables will be turned. The Scripture says in many places throughout the Proverbs, the Prophecies and in the Revelation that those who inflict ruin and misery on others will, in fact, suffer those things themselves in eternity.

Verse 18 says, "There is no fear of God before their eyes." No fear of God. How many of us have a true fear of God? I don't mean being afraid because we know we've sinned and expect punishment like a father who would correct his child and the child would be fearful before the father, afraid of being slapped up side the head, receiving a 2x4 on his butt, or whatever. I don't mean that kind of fear, but the kind of fear that says, "I'm not worthy to be in the presence of

God." That reverential fear that says, "God is so awesome, so great, so beautiful, so incomprehensible and here I am, a sinful human." That kind of fear or awe that says, I respect God for who He is. I'm afraid to be in God's presence because I'm so dirty and filthy. Like Isaiah said when God commissioned him to be a prophet, "I can't stand before you, God. I'm unclean. I've said a lot of bad things." Later on in his book Isaiah says all of us, all of our lives before God look like filthy rags.

There's no fear of God, generally speaking. Everyone who does not fear and respect God is sinning. That encompasses every person that we know, especially that person we see in our mirror. We recognize that there are no exceptions. People sin.

Then Paul addresses in these last two verses the purpose of the Law.

Now the Jews, we know, had gotten confused about its purpose. Many people today also are confused in the same way. What was the purpose of the Law? Was it not given so we could live righteously and to be accepted by God?

Well, Paul says here to those who are under the Law, if you live under the Law, what the law says is what you have to go by and you will be judged for that. To those outside the Law (as he talked about earlier in this letter) he says, you are still accountable to God because of your conscience. You have to live by your conscience that is put there by God and is accepted by the Holy Spirit.

The purpose of the Law, Paul tells us here, is to make sin obvious. If you don't know what's expected of you, you don't know when you're missing those expectations. When you go to work for someone, your boss or the people who hired you should relate to you what's expected from you on your job. If you're working in a doctor's office and you're supposed to keep accurate records, when the doctor looks on someone's chart, he or she is expecting those records to be there, complete and accurate. That is what is expected of you. Now for example, you say, "I'm just going to write an outline, I know what I'm talking about. I know whom he visited on Thursday. I'll just put his name down, with the date and what he came in for. The doctor will know."

Two months later the doctor checks the chart and says, "What's this? It doesn't give the diagnosis. It doesn't give the medication. It doesn't say if or when he is supposed to come back. What's going on here?"

Someone, *you*, didn't meet the expectations. So you see that the purpose of the rules is to show when we fall short. Rules of conduct act as a standard or a measuring guide to go by.

I read a story about a town that wanted to set up a police force for the first time. So they advertised for candidates, listing the criteria needed to qualify to be an officer. You had to have three letters of recommendation, you had to have a good work history, you had to be a resident in town and you had to be at least six feet tall.

A bunch of guys lined up at the door waiting to go in for the interview. Two of them were talking. One of them said, "I've got a letter from the mayor, a letter from the governor, and all my work history."

The second man says, "Well, I don't have those, but I've got a good work history and connections in the mayor's office. I know people."

The first one goes in, and the recruiter looks over all his

information. Then he says, "I want you to step up to that chart to be sure you measure up." He passed.

The second one says, "Well, that's no problem. I've got all the same criteria he does."

The recruiter looks over his paperwork. That's all fine and in order. The candidate stepped up to the measuring chart. His height was a half-inch short. In spite of his excellent credentials the recruiter had to reject his application.

Rules are there as guidelines. The Law was given as a guideline to show where we fall short. God never intended the Israelites or anybody following Him to live strictly by the commandments He gave at Sinai, or all the multiple hundreds that came afterward. God never intended for us to live by the letter of the Law, but rather, the Spirit of the Law, as Paul says in another place (2 Corinthians 3:6).

The rules of conduct in themselves do not make us righteous. You could follow every rule in the book, and you still would not be righteous because you would still be a sinner. There would still be a rule somewhere that you missed causing you to fall short. It is through the Law that we become conscious of sin.

It's like a child living with a family who is not a true member of that family. That child is not a full member until he is adopted. A child can receive love, live with a family, and be in a family all his life, but legally he is not a part of the family until he is adopted. Even though he might be the most obedient child, the most well behaved child that you and I know. Even though it seems he does everything the parents expect of him, he is not a legal member of the family. Until the adoption happens, he is still an outsider. He is still a person with a need.

We all are outside the family of God until we recognize we are sinners and take the step of faith. Paul is saying here that our conclusion from this discussion of who is acceptable to God is *no one*. Not one of us is righteousness in our own right. Not one of us is without sin. As Jesus reminded the people who gathered around a woman caught in adultery, "The one of you who is without sin, you cast the first stone," (John 8:7). They all disappeared because they all knew they were sinners. Since we all recognize that the Scriptures point out that we are all under sin, none of us have righteousness of our own. We need help. We need a Savior.

To sum it up, verse 23 states, "All have sinned and come short of the glory of God." Verse 24 is the rest of the sentence, which most people don't quote, "and are justified freely by his grace through the redemption that comes through Christ Jesus."

All have an opportunity to be forgiven, to be saved, to be adopted into God's family. Where are you today? I pray that you have recognized your sinful state and come to God for grace and forgiveness. I pray that you are living for Him today rather than for yourself. Never forget that you are no exception to the charge that all people are sinful people. You need forgiveness now and you will need forgiveness every time you realize you have sinned.

CHAPTER 7

One Single Step

Today's Bible Reading: Romans 3:21-31

But now a righteousness from God, apart
from the Law, has been made known, to
which the Law and the Prophets testify.
This righteousness from God comes through
faith in Jesus Christ to all who believe.
There is no difference, for all have sinned
and fall short of the glory of God, and are
justified freely by his grace through the
redemption that came by Christ Jesus.
—Romans 3:21-24

Many of you probably have received advertisements in the
mail where, if you buy one item, you'll get bonus items. One,
two, three, four or more things are thrown in as bonuses for
free, so they say. You order the main item, and you get more
than you've asked for.

In this first part of this letter that Paul wrote to the
church at Rome, he has already explained carefully to four

different types of people that salvation is by faith alone. It is not by works. It is not by any other means. It is by faith alone. When you exercise faith in Jesus Christ, you are then saved from the punishment your sins deserve. You are saved *from* eternal destruction in hell, and you have been saved *to* an eternal life with God.

But more than that comes in the package. In most of the rest of the letter Paul talks about three other things that are included for free when you get the main item of salvation.

Here in this lesson, as well as the next few, we're going to talk about the first bonus, righteousness that comes through faith.

Paul interchanges the words *righteousness* and *justification* in this passage. He says:

> Our *righteousness* from God apart from the Law has been made known to which the Law and the Prophets testify, *this righteousness* comes from God through faith in Jesus Christ to all who believe. There is no difference, for all have sinned and fall short of the glory of God and are *justified* freely by his grace through the redemption that came by Christ Jesus. God presented him as a sacrifice of atonement through faith in his blood. He did this to demonstrate his justice because in his forbearance he had left the sins committed beforehand unpunished. He did it to demonstrate His justice at the present time so as to be just and *the One who justifies* those who have faith in Jesus."
>
> Romans 3:21-26 (Emphasis mine).

What is Paul saying here? You have been saved by faith, but in addition to that, you have been justified. You have been made righteous, that is, when you stand before the Judge, he can say to you, "I find no fault in you. You do not deserve to be punished."

How do we get this justification? How do we get this righteousness, this position of being right before God? It comes by faith alone, not by the Law (v. 21). It is apart from the Law. The Law can't provide it. We can never be good enough to please God because we're not perfect. If we were perfect we would be God. But we're not God, and we can never be good enough either by living by the Law of the Old Testament or by living by any creed that is presented by any church. We can't be good enough. We can't do it that way because we're natural sinners, because we tend to be sinful.

"There's none righteous, no not one," the Scripture says, except Jesus. You can never be good enough to please God by your actions. But you can be good enough to please God simply by faith, simply by placing your faith, as Paul says here, in the blood of Jesus which was shed for you, that blood which washes away your sins, that blood which makes you clean before God. You can achieve this position with God simply by faith. You must believe it in your head and you must act like you believe it. If a person really doesn't understand or really doesn't believe, he can't act. If someone truly believes something he's going to act like he does.

For those of you reading this who are married, if you truly love your spouse, you will act like it. If someone is married to someone they really don't like, it shows, doesn't it? We've seen and we know marriages like that.

If we truly believe that Jesus has forgiven us, has done away with our sins, we will act like we're living a victorious life. We will live with joy; we will live with grace and blessing because those are the things that God has given to us.

That's an important note: It's what God has done for us. We couldn't do it. We can't earn it. We can't be good enough. Paul says this all came about because God presented Jesus as a sacrifice for us to demonstrate His justice. You see, when Jesus hung on the cross, his hands, feet and side were pierced, and his blood flowed; that was a sacrifice made for you and me. That was the atonement for our sin, which only had to be made once. He did it to prove He is the One who can do that.

This salvation and this righteousness is available to us because of God's acts of mercy, grace and love. It's all He and not we. It's all God and not me. I can't do it. He must do it for me.

So where does that leave us? (v. 27) "Where then is boasting?" Who can go around and say, "I am righteous. I am good enough for God. I have made it?" No one can, not me, not you. You cannot ever tell yourself or anyone else truthfully that you are accepted by God based on how you live or what you have done. It doesn't work that way.

Boasting is excluded, Paul says, simply because you didn't do anything. How can you boast in something you haven't done? If you didn't do it, you can't brag about it.

If someone else did it for you or to you, you should be bragging up that person. So our lives should be exemplified by praising God, thanking God, and pointing other people to God because He is our (and their) source of hope. We should be praising God for giving us this righteousness, this hope, this joy that we have.

Then Paul goes on to ask, "Is this limited only to Jews?

Is God only the God of Jews?" They were given the Law. They were given special privileges in the Old Testament as God's people, as God's agency in the world. Is he the God of the Jews only? His conclusion is no.

He can't be God only to the Jews if salvation and righteousness come by faith alone, apart from the Law. That opens it up to everybody. If it's not limited to the Law, which the Jews had exclusive claim on, it's open to everybody, because it's not dependent on the Law. God is God of all because anyone can be a child of God by faith. Faith in God is not dependent on any creed that is invented by man or any declaration made by any church or group.

There are many denominations (church groups that have a common set of creeds or beliefs) in the world all claiming to be Christian. There are organizations and ministries all over the world claiming to be right and each one has their own set of doctrines that they believe and teach. How dependent should we be on those creeds? They are important, but they don't save. Only faith in Christ saves. Only faith in Christ makes us righteous.

Does citizenship make us righteous? If we have Jewish history or heritage does that make us special? If we were born and raised in a Christian church and a Christian family does that make us special? No. None of those things can offer us any hope other than steer us toward a faith in Christ. Faith cannot be inherited. Each individual must express it for himself.

No other criteria that we can set or that is set by men can save us, either. Do you have to be baptized? Do you have to be a member of a church? Do you have to do this or that? No. You are saved and you are made righteous, justified before God only by faith. Salvation is by faith alone. Righteousness is by faith alone.

Do we nullify the Law just because we shouldn't depend on it for our salvation? No. As we mentioned a couple of lessons ago and Paul reminds us again, we don't destroy the Law, we don't eliminate that, but instead we put it in its proper place. The Law was given as a guide to direct men to God; to get their focus on God, not to save them. Salvation is by faith.

Paul is going to go into that subject in more detail by showing an example from the life of Abraham. He too, was saved, but the Law didn't save him. We're going to talk about that in the next lesson.

What Paul is saying in these couple of paragraphs is, you are saved by faith and because you are saved by faith, part of the package is that you are also made righteous by faith. You are made clean before God, and when you stand before Him at the judgment, He will say, "Welcome, faithful servant." He will also say those wonderful words, "You are not in danger of any punishment."

But in order to be righteous before God, you must first be saved by God. So we go back to the main question. Have you been saved? Have you put your faith in Jesus Christ to deal with the sin that's in your life? Have you asked Him to be your Lord and Savior? That is the first and most important step. One simple step will change your life forever. I pray that you have.

CHAPTER 8

"Abraham, Father of Our Faith"

Today's Bible Reading: Romans 4:1-25

Now when a man works, his wages are not
credited to him as a gift, but as an obligation.
However, to the man who does not work
but trusts God who justifies the wicked,
his faith is credited as righteousness.
—Romans 4:4, 5

All his life Fred had been told that his family was descended from European aristocracy. Somewhere in their family tree were kings and princes of Europe. Someplace, perhaps in France, Italy or maybe England someone or several people had been involved in history at the highest level.

Out of curiosity, he said, "I guess I'll do a little genealogical research to see if the rumor is true. So he started checking, and before he got back very many generations in his family tree he discovered that instead of his roots going back to Europe, they went toward the Middle East.

People in his line, instead of being European ancestors were Arabian bedouins. That was a disappointment for Fred.

Our heritage is the focus of this lesson. What is our spiritual heritage? Where does it come from? Is it of any value? Whom can we claim as members of our spiritual family tree?

If you ask a Muslim where their faith began, he'll tell you that they trace their beginnings back through Mohammed to Abraham. If you ask a Jew who the father of their faith system is, he'll take you back through the prophets to Moses and back to Abraham.

I don't think it was a mistake that Paul used Abraham as the example to hold up to these people in Rome. Abraham symbolized not only the Jewish heritage, but the Gentile as well. People from other systems besides the Jews could go back to Abraham and claim him as the father of their faith.

So Paul opens the chapter by asking this question, "What shall we say that Abraham, our father discovered in this matter of faith?" To rephrase it, "What did Abraham learn in his lifetime regarding faith?" By looking at his example, we learn three lessons that Abraham either learned or illustrated by his life that we can draw from to find out where faith fits into the picture.

First, Paul says that Abraham was justified by faith, not by works, which we have already discussed, but now we see Abraham as a classic example.

If, in fact, Abraham was justified by works, says Paul (v. 2), he had something to brag about. If works could have justified Abraham he would be a prime example. He had plenty of things he did that were good and right in the sight of God. These things could have earned him credit to save him and to make him righteous, but God's system doesn't work that way. Abraham could have been justified, if that is the way it works, but it isn't. If anyone could have earned his righteousness, it would have been Abraham.

Abraham could have boasted to other people about all the things he did if he was so inclined, but not before God, because God does not look at works, he looks at the heart. He asks how faithful you are, not how hard you worked. He doesn't care how much you have accomplished.

People today sometimes will say, "I know so-and-so is such a good man. He does so many wonderful things for the church, the community, and his family." He may be a wonderful guy, but not before God. He can't earn his righteousness.

God says, "You can be the best person in your community. You can be the most respected, the most well liked character on the whole block, and still go to hell. You will still be lost." No matter how much we do or how well we behave, we cannot earn our way.

Paul says (v. 4) the reason is that, if you earn your way, if you work to try to please God, everything God does for you is just payment for your work. He's just paying you what you deserve for working so hard.

It's like each of us, when we go to our jobs. We expect payment for our services. Working at a restaurant, selling groceries, installing phone lines or whatever it is are things we expect to get paid for, right? We're not going to break our backs for somebody else and not get paid for it.

But no matter how well we do our jobs a judge is not going to let us off if we are guilty of breaking the law. No one is above the law or immune to the law. We could be the best chef in town, but if we have been caught speeding, we still owe the fine.

Paul's simply saying here, "Look, if you think you're going to work for God, that's well and good, work for God. What you get is a result of that work, but the results don't make you right before God. It just makes you feel a little better because you did what you knew was right, but that doesn't change your standing before God. You are still a sinner in need of a Savior. Faith is what is credited to you as righteousness."

So Abraham is given as an example of someone who could have been declared righteous by his works, but he wasn't. He was declared righteous by faith.

Paul goes on to say that Abraham could also have been declared righteous because he was circumcised. But that isn't what it takes, either. He didn't get circumcised in order to be right with God. He didn't get circumcised to make himself more righteous. He didn't get circumcised because that was the thing to do. He got circumcised because God instructed him to do that *as a result* of his faith. This was something God asked him and his family to do to set them apart as faithful people. It was a mark of their faithfulness.

Paul simply asks the question. "Let's look at this logically," he says. "Was Abraham faithful before he was circumcised or after?" The answer is *before*. Circumcision had nothing to do with it. He remained faithful afterward, but that was not what created his standing with God. He was credited as being faithful long before he was circumcised.

That means no matter what the church might impose as a ritual or formality, whether it is baptism or any other kind of ceremony, none of that will change your position with God. None of that will make you more faithful. None of that will make you more righteous before God. Only your faith in God will make you right with God.

Let's not confuse the two. Let's not think that being baptized or going through any other ceremony that a church might require will make us better Christians; it won't. You're still subject to sin and temptation. Don't forget that. You're still in need of daily confession for those things that come your way. Don't forget that either. No ritual imposed by anyone will make you right before God.

As a Christian church we ask people to be baptized, not because it makes them perfect, not because it makes them right, not because of any special blessing, but as a seal of confirmation of their faith. They declare to the world through everybody who witnesses the event that they have pledged their faith in Almighty God. The God we serve as a church is the God they choose to follow.

So, we've seen so far that Abraham was justified, not by works, not by ceremony and thirdly, Paul goes on to say (v. 13), neither was it by law.

Abraham was justified by faith, not by law. for three logical reasons. First of all, the formal Law had not been given. That didn't come until Moses was on the scene many years later. The Law was not even there at the time of Abraham. There was no written code. Abraham simply heard the word of God, understood the presence of God, and was faithful to God without the Law, without any list of do's and don'ts, without any standard or formal law. Abraham was simply faithful because he had found God faithful to him.

Second, Paul says in verse 14, those who live by the

law are heirs of wrath. Faith has no value, and the promise is worthless; because law brings wrath, and where there is no law there is no transgression. It goes back to the point he made back in chapter 3 where he said the purpose of the law is not to save us, but to point out how far from God's righteousness we really are, how far from perfection we really fall. God sets up standards. The Law is there to show us we can't meet those standards. It's simply there as a guideline for living. None of us can do it perfectly. None of us can keep the whole law. As Jesus said, "If you break one Law, you are guilty of them all." So we are guilty.

The Law is there, not to save us, not to make us righteous, but to point out to us how far short of the target we fall. That's its purpose. That's one of the reasons God gave it.

It does not bring hope. The Law does not bring hope because if you break the Law, instead of hope you get punishment. Just like the laws on our civil law books. They are not there to praise us for the good things we do. They are there to punish us for the wrong things we do. If we break the law we expect to go to court and receive a fine or whatever the penalty might be. It doesn't offer hope. Instead, it offers punishment.

Faith offers hope. Faith placed in a God who is patient, loving, and willing to forgive gives us hope. That's the final point Paul makes regarding Abraham's faith.

Abraham's faith was placed in the living God (v. 17), who gives life to the dead and calls things that are not as though they were. Abraham trusted this God whom he knew and recognized as the Creator. This God called things into being as we read in Genesis 1. He spoke; it happened. Abraham believed that God.

What had God told Abraham? You will be the father of many nations through a son born in old age. Abraham believed that. Abraham really believed that, and yet he was willing to follow in obedience all the way to the sacrificial altar, knowing that this God who had created the whole world, who had sustained the world up to that point and who was a God who had proven his faithfulness, this same God, if necessary, would return his son from the dead. That's the kind of faith Abraham had. That's the kind of faith that made him righteous before God. That is what God credited to him as righteousness. It was his faith. It was not anything he had done. Everything he did was a result of this faith. It was not in circumcision, because he was circumcised, not to make himself righteous, but as a seal of this faith. It was not because he followed any code, written down or passed down as a law to be obeyed. It was simply his faith.

Abraham is properly called the father of our faith. Because of him we see that righteousness could not have come by works, ritual, or the law. We can never brag about or take pride in our standing with Christ. Our position in Him is a gift, given to us freely by faith. We cannot earn it. Neither can we achieve righteousness by performing any ritual imposed by a church or other group. Church membership, baptism, ritual washing, or any other ceremony or act doesn't make you righteous before God either. None of these things will do that apart from faith. Nor can we be made faithful by the law. Trying to live by a code of law, trying to live righteously will only fail. Faith in God, through the power of the Holy Spirit and His Son, Jesus, is all that is necessary. Nothing more.

Friend, I ask you to look at yourself right now. Are

you living by faith or are you trying to please the Lord by your lifestyle and behavior? Do you trust in your church membership, baptism, or acceptance by others? Set all that aside. Learn to trust the Lord by faith. Go to Him right now and confess that you cannot make yourself righteous before God and you need help. You just need the assurance that faith is enough!

CHAPTER 9

I'm So Happy, I'm Speechless

Today's Bible Reading: Romans 5:1-11

For if, when we were God's enemies, we
were reconciled to him through the death
of his Son, how much more, having been
reconciled, shall we be saved through his life!
—Romans 5:10

I want to begin by telling you a story. I would like to tell you
a story that I think illustrates what Paul is going to say in the
passage that we're going to look at in this lesson.

Terry was a fifteen-year-old girl living at home with her
mom who was a single mother. Terry and her mom had
different ideas on how her life should be run. Terry was not
happy with the way her mother asked her to do things or
insisted on doing things. Her mother's rules at home were
tough.

She wanted to be free. She wanted to dress the way she
wanted. She wanted to go with the friends that she liked.

She wanted to be free to be herself, and her mother tried, as most mothers do, to keep a lid on that, to keep her under control.

Finally, after many times of arguing, fighting, and bickering, Terry left home. She ran away and went to a city some distance away where she thought her mother would never find her because the disagreement was so great.

For a while she lived the way she wanted. She found friends. She found housing. She found a job. She thought things were going well. She lived her life her way, doing the things she thought were fun.

After a while Terry was going places in her career. She had the resources and the time to go out partying, often and long. She could come and go as she pleased.

What she didn't know was that her mother had a close friend who found her in that city. She found out where Terry lived and sent her address back home to her mother. Her mother's friend, Margaret, kept a close eye on Terry without her knowing it. She didn't spy on her every move, but she knew where she lived and her general movements.

Her mother would occasionally send her a card or a brief note saying, "Terry, I love you. Please come home." Terry never knew that, because every time she would receive something from her mother she would rip it up and throw it into the garbage without even reading it. She would not have anything to do with her mother. Her roommate even thought that was rather extreme.

One day Margaret ran into Terry on the street, and she, too, reminded her of her mother's love. But Terry rejected it. She didn't want it. She wanted to be herself. She wanted to stay as she was. Everything was going well.

Or so she thought.

Then all of a sudden her world changed. Her roommate moved out and left her with the total responsibility for the rent, which she couldn't afford so she lost her apartment.

Because she didn't have a place to stay, she couldn't keep herself clean; so she lost her job. She was living on the street in her car, which she was struggling to pay for. Her residence consisted of moving from one parking lot to another each night, being kicked out by the police early in the morning.

She became destitute, homeless, and hungry.

Margaret found her again on the street and talked to her. Terry still did not want to go home. She still insisted she could work things out and things would be all right.

Finally, one night she gave in and said, "This is it. It's hopeless. I can't find a job. I have no home. It's no use in me even living." She went to the nearest drug store and bought a large bottle of pills.

Margaret was outside the door when she came out and tried to stop her. She did at least convince Terry to call home and talk to her mother.

So Terry went to the phone booth with Margaret at her side. Margaret agreed to pay for the call. Terry dialed the number of her mother's house. She got the answering machine. She heard her mother's voice saying, "I'm sorry. I'm not home right now, but if you're Terry, I love you. Please come home."

Terry slammed down the receiver and left the phone booth. She felt rejected one more time. She went off by herself and swallowed the pills.

A short time later she was found by someone and rushed

to the hospital. When she opened her eyes, lying in her hospital bed, the first person she saw was Margaret.

"What are you doing here?"

Margaret says, "Terry, you know your mother loves you. You know, as your mother's friend, I love you. We don't want you to die. We love you, and we'd like for you to go home when you get out of this place."

Finally she convinced Terry to call home once more, and her mother was there waiting for the call. They talked briefly on the phone. Among the three of them they arrange for Terry to go home. Margaret was willing to pay the fare, even though it cost her dearly for the price of the fare. She sold her car to get the money to send Terry home.

When Terry got there, her mother was right there, ready and waiting. They had a joyous reunion.

Terry forgot momentarily how bad she had felt to live at home. To know that her mother loved her enough to receive her back in spite of all she had done, made all the hurts of the past recede into a distant memory

Terry kept saying over and over, "I'm sorry, Mom. I'm sorry for what I've done. Please forgive me."

Her mother said, "Terry, you're forgiven. I love you. Welcome home."

Sometimes they would just cry on each others shoulders, because they couldn't speak, they were so happy and relieved.

Isaiah 53:6 says, "We have all gone our own way. In spite of what God has done for us, every one of us has gone our own way."

That brings us back to our passage here in Romans. Paul has already set the stage in the early part of the book. He said everyone has gone his or her own way. They've done their own thing. They have rebelled against God. God in his love sent his Son to restore them to himself. All they need to do is ask forgiveness and say, "Lord, I'm sorry. Please forgive me and welcome me back." If you do that with faith, Paul says, God will welcome you with open arms.

Then, coming to chapter 5, he says, "Therefore, since we have been justified through faith we have been forgiven by faith. We have peace with God through our Lord Jesus Christ, through whom we have gained access by faith into this grace in which we now stand. And we rejoice in the hope of the glory of God."

There is now a grand reunion between the people who have gone astray and the God who loves them. There is a reunion of souls so great, so wondrous, Paul says that we rejoice. We give God the glory. We rejoice in what he has done for us through Christ. We rejoice in the hope of the glory of God, not only so, but we rejoice in our sufferings, all we had to go through. We thank God for that because that brought us to the position where we see we needed His help.

We can be reunited with the God who loves us, because God has poured out his love in our hearts by the Holy Spirit whom he has given us. That's the friend who stands by us no matter what happens. That's the friend who comes to us in our state of rebellion and says, "God loves you. Please come back." That's the friend you need.

"You see," Paul says, "at just the right time. Just the moment we needed Him when we were still powerless, Christ died for the ungodly."

To the person who strayed from God, the one who knew God was there all along, the one who knew God loved him and walked away anyway, God said, "I love you enough to sacrifice my son for you."

He didn't wait until the person was ready for a reunion. He went ahead and gave the sacrifice then, so the reunion might be greater. God demonstrates his own love for us in this, that while we were still sinners, Christ died for us. It's a wonderful truth. God took the initiative. He made the sacrifice. He paid the fare home. All we have to do is take the plane by faith.

> Since we have been justified, since we have been forgiven, we have now been made right by his blood, how much more can we be saved by His life? For if, when we were God's enemies, we were reconciled to Him through the death of His son, how much more, having been reconciled, shall we be saved through his life? Not only is this so, we also rejoice in God through Jesus Christ, through whom we have now received reconciliation.
>
> Romans 5:9-11

We should rejoice. We should be excited. We should be praising God every day, because he rescued us from that life of sin, that life of rebellion, that life of doing things our own way, which only leads to destruction.

When we're saved there is a grand reunion between a lost soul and the God who created it, between the rebellious soul and the God of love. That is the most wonderful kind of reunion there can be. Sometimes, when I reflect on that fact I become so awe-filled, knowing that Christ did this for me. I think about it. I meditate on it, and all I can say is, "Thank you, Jesus. Thank you for bringing me home."

How about you? Have you gone home again and asked the Father to take you in? He will, you know. No matter what you have done. No matter how far you have run or to what depths of degradation you have taken yourself, you are never out of the reach of God's love.

Like Terry, all you have to do is call. He'll be there to receive you and to set you right again. Won't you do that today?

CHAPTER 10

Breaking the Curse

Today's Bible Reading: Romans 5:12-21

Consequently, just as the result of one
trespass was condemnation for all men, so
also the result of one act of righteousness
was justification that brings life for all men.
For just as though the disobedience of the
one man the many were made sinners,
so also through the obedience of the one
man the many will be made righteous.
—Romans 5:18, 19

New Tribes Mission has a video called "E-Tau." Perhaps you
have seen it. This video tells the story of a missionary couple
who went to a particular group of people and spent more
than fourteen years learning the language and the culture
of the people. They finally got to the point where they could
teach them the Bible.

They began with Adam, back in Genesis, and progressed
through, explaining in every detail about how God created

the world perfect, Adam caused sin to come into the world, and since then everyone is a sinner, including the people of that particular tribe. Then they got to the point where they could explain the acts of Jesus; what he did, why he did it, and the fact that they could be free from their sin simply by faith.

When they understood the truth of what Jesus had done, what happened? They broke out in a joyous celebration. They had a huge village party that lasted for more than two hours one afternoon and they continue to celebrate even today.

Knowing and believing that Christ suffered, died and rose again for them made the difference. It released them from all guilt, the bondage of sin, and false worship, to a spirit of celebration. They were able to personalize the message.

Well, in the first half of this chapter, Paul talks about that kind of joyous celebration. We can celebrate because of what Christ has done for us as individuals. What he did on the cross brings hope and brings freedom from sin. Paul makes the point that this God, who did all this, is not the God of America, as a lot of people tend to think. It's not the God of the Jews, not the God of the Europeans. Anyone, anywhere has access to the love of God through faith.

Paul, like the missionaries I mentioned, goes all the way back to Adam to show us what God has done for us. He starts verse 12 by saying, "Therefore just as sin entered the world through one man - —that act was reversed by one man, Jesus Christ."

He first discusses the fact that all are under sin because of what Adam did. Sin came into the world through one man, and we're all familiar with the story back in Genesis

3. God gave one simple command to Adam and Eve. He put them in the garden, asked them to take care of it, and to worship Him. They were to be his companions here on earth. He said, "I just give you one command. Don't eat of the one tree in the middle of the garden. That is a sacred tree." They couldn't even keep the one command. They broke it. They ate and because of that God expelled them from the garden and the rest, as they say, is history.

So all people in the world are sinners simply because of what Adam did. He initiated sin, and it has gone through the whole world since then. It's called "original sin" because we're all born in it.

But all people also, as each of us can testify, sin on our own. All of us have done things that we know violated a rule, a command, or a principle. Therefore we know we have sinned. Each of us knows we have sinned intentionally. Other times we sin by omission. That is, we didn't knowingly break a rule or law, but we failed to do what we knew was the right thing under the circumstances. (See James 4:15) In any case, we know that we have sinned. Paul has already mentioned that two or three times in this letter. "All have sinned." By actions or by inactions we know when we have done something wrong.

In another place he said that both Jews and Gentiles are sinners, making sure most people understood that this was not just a Jewish thing but Gentiles are included as well. People everywhere are sinners. He also reminds us that because of sin (by the way, not only Paul but other people remind us as well) we stand under judgment. Over in chapter 6 he's going to say, "The wages of sin is death." That's the judgment of God. Physically and spiritually we stand under judgment. Jesus said in John, chapter 3, "If you have rejected me; if you have not accepted the Son by faith, you're still under the judgment of God," (v. 18).

So all people are sinners as a result of what Adam did, but yet we're also sinners in our own right. Paul said that sin reigned from the time of Adam to Moses. Everybody was a sinner. Now we know there was no Savior at that time. And, yet, he tells us we can find from the early records that people were made righteous before God by faith. Although they didn't have the Law, it was still possible to please God.

Three examples are Enoch, Noah and Abraham. Enoch walked with God, and God took him (Genesis 5:24). "Noah found grace in the eyes of the Lord" as the little children's song says. God blessed Noah. God used Noah to preserve humanity when God brought judgment on the world (Genesis 6:1-7:22). Later on, the story of Abraham tells how he migrated from the area of the Chaldeans (or Babylonians) and made his way down into the Canaan area. In obedience to God he lived by faith his whole life, and he pleased God. These men are prime examples of pleasing God by faith, not by law or works. They, too, were sinners but found that faith overcomes sin.

So, all of us are sinners, yet even in spite of that, we can still please God, if we live by faith. Anybody can do that. You don't have to be Jewish. You don't have to be European. You don't have to be brought up in a church. You don't have to be anybody special. You just have to be alive and breathing and have the ability to reason.

In verses 15-19, Paul tells us that the gift of justification (or righteousness) reverses the sin of Adam on our behalf. Adam initiated sin, and it spread throughout the world through propagation. Every child since then has been born in sin. That is, each one of us, as we are born, adds to the numbers that are sinners. But when Christ came, He brought a gift that corrected all that. He's the one who provided the sacrifice and ability to go back to God through faith.

People become Christians one by one, the way they do to become sinners. Christianity, by the grace of God, has spread widely all over the world. It started out with one man who taught twelve. The group increased to 120. That one hundred twenty soon became more than five thousand. We know that whole villages often come to Christ where missionaries are working. We know that sometimes a revival occurs in certain areas. An explosion of evangelism occurs in certain pockets of our world. But in spite of these events, it is still one soul at a time.

The first man brought condemnation, Paul says. When Adam sinned he brought condemnation on each one of us. We are under God's judgment, but the second man, Jesus Christ brings forgiveness. He brings hope. He brings reconciliation or righteousness. There was one man in each case; one condemned us, the other forgave us.

In his final point he says the first one brought death. Verse 21 in our passage says, "Just as sinned reigned in death, so also grace might reign through righteousness." None of us, I suppose, can imagine what it is like to sit on death row. Obviously, because we're here we haven't been executed. But can you imagine the mental anguish that some of these men and women go through while they are waiting for their final moment, knowing that they have been found guilty, judged by their peers and sentenced with no reprieve. The only hope for such a person is a governor's pardon which is rarely granted.

We may not be on death row physically, yet all of us are in a similar condition spiritually until we get to the point where we cry out to God and say, "Forgive me, God."

Jesus wants to set us free. Jesus, in His name and through the gift of grace, wants to set us free. You don't have to die spiritually. "I've already died for you. I've already taken your place in the execution. You don't have to. Just accept my gift of grace, faith, and righteousness," Jesus says.

Then Paul adds, as he does in each of these discussions, the relationship of the law to this subject. Why was the law added? Why did that even come along? Why did God bother to give Moses the Ten Commandments and all the others that were added later?

Well, as we have seen before, the law was given for at least one purpose, to expose our sinfulness. It makes us aware how really bad we are so we can come to God and admit our sinfulness. It causes us to admit that we can't make it to heaven on our own. In these verses, he says the law was added so you will be more aware of how sinful you are. A literal way of reading it is "that sin might increase." It doesn't mean that we become more sinful, but that we would be more exposed or more knowledgeable of how sinful we are. When we see ourselves as being, as Isaiah says, "filthy rags" in God's sight, then when we receive the gift of grace. How much more precious that is.

If we see ourselves as being hopeless or helpless, and someone comes along and gives us a gift that helps us out of our hopeless state, it restores us to a place of dignity and hope. How precious that gift is! How much more precious it is to those who see their desperate plight than to those who don't understand.

Paul repeats himself several times on certain points because they are important points. The gift of justification, that gift that we've been talking about back a few chapters is that gift that comes by the grace of God. It comes from the God that says, "If you've accepted Christ by faith, I'm also going to give you this gift so that when I look at you I see no sin. I see nothing worthy of judgment. I see you as standing before Me and you're okay. You're all right! You're acceptable before me because of what Christ has done and you've put your faith in Him."

God offers this gift to anyone out there in the whole wide world. Paul says in verse 17, "Those who receive God's gift" or "Anybody willing to receive the gift." In verse 18 he says justification comes on all men if they are willing to receive him. And then down in verse 19 he says, "the many." All those who are willing are made righteous. Three times he repeats that point.

So even though you were born in sin because of what Adam did, way, way back at the beginning and even though you have committed sins in your own right, you can be set free from the bondage, the penalty, the curse of sin and made right with God simply by faith, simply by believing the promises of God, then going out and living like you believe it.

Don't live in despair and despondency any more. Live with joy. Live with happiness. Celebrate what Christ has done for you; it's something to rejoice in. You didn't do it, Christ did.

Adam put you under the curse, but Christ broke the curse. Praise God!

If you've never done it before, now is a good time to take that step of faith. Confess your sinfulness to God and receive his forgiveness and experience the freedom he offers you. To think you can be free from the curse, just for the asking!

CHAPTER 11

The Tape Has Been Erased

Today's Bible Reading: Romans 6:1-14

What shall we say then? Shall we go
on sinning so that grace may increase?
By no means! We died to sin; how
can we live in it any longer?
—Romans 6:1, 2

Billy Graham says he carries around with him a little portable cassette recorder so that if he has a sermon idea or a note or letter he wants to dictate, he can just stop and dictate into the machine and pass it to his secretary for transcribing later. He also reminds us that with this machine he can quickly erase anything he has recorded if he changes his mind or if he wants to amend it in any way.

Our lives are like a recording machine in the hands of God because everything we do, everything we say is put on record. God keeps track. That record can and will be, as the police are accustomed to saying, used against us in a court of law—the highest court ever—the judgment seat of Christ except for the fact that we who have come to Christ by faith for salvation have had the tape wiped clean. If we placed our faith in the sacrificial death of Jesus, if we trust him for salvation and for justification, as Paul has been talking about, then we have been made clean. Our tape has been erased.

That erasure also makes us sanctified, which is the subject Paul is leading into in this lesson and we will be discussing in the next two or three. That means, in simple terms, we are made clean. We are made special. Sometimes that is referred to as being set apart or being made holy before God. That is what we are.

As Paul introduces his subject he asks two rhetorical questions. One is here in chapter 6:1, which we'll discuss today. Another is in verse 15 which we will look at in the next lesson.

The first question he asks, by way of introduction to his subject is: "What shall we say then? Should we go on sinning so that grace may increase?"

Now remember back in chapter 3:7, 8, Paul already asked this question once and said no, you shouldn't do that because that's not prudent, that's not right, that's not a good reason for sinning, to make God look good.

Now he's going to answer it in a different way. He's going to answer by saying you shouldn't have sin in your life because when you became saved you also became sanctified, set apart, made holy, made different. Your old life is gone, and you're starting over. You don't start over with the same problems you had before.

He says, "We died to sin, so how can we live in it any longer?" He answered the question with a question.

If somebody's dead, what is he capable of doing? Nothing. Paul says if you're dead, you're not able to sin. Physically if you're dead, it's over. What you have done in your past will be judged, but that's it. As Hebrews 9:25 says, "Once you die, the next thing you're going to do is face the judgment."

When you put your faith in Jesus Christ you died. Your old self, your spiritual life, which was nothing before or very meager and was distracted by false teaching, is dead. You buried all that when you put your faith in Christ. You were crucified with him. You were buried with him. So the old life is gone with all its sin, with all its baggage, with all its dirty stuff. It's gone. Your tape has been erased.

Since we died with Christ in his death, sin should have no more control over us. Sin should not be evident in our lives, because we're starting over with a clean slate. The control of sin has been destroyed. We are free to please God in our lives.

But, if we died with Christ, Paul says, we don't remain dead. We are also raised with him as well to a new life, a new life that is characterized by serving God. He says (verse 10), "jJust as Christ lived his life to please God, (verse 11) so should you." Your life should be characterized by pleasing God.

Now here are some facts about Christ that he deals with. First Christ died, he was buried, and he was resurrected never to die again. It only happened once. A person can only die once. Jesus was physical, he was human while he was here on the earth, and once he died that was it. He could never do it again.

When he rose from the grave, he conquered death. He proved that he was more powerful than death and death can never grab him again. It can never destroy his body again. So when he died, he died to destroy death and sin. In verse 10, Paul says, "Christ died to sin once for all." Once for all. That's it. No repeats.

Now you can read that two ways and both ways are proper. *Once*, Christ died *once* for all people who are willing to place their faith in him. This is true because we know that God accepts anybody who comes to Christ by faith. We know this is true because Jesus himself holds out the invitation, "Come unto me and I will give you rest." Hebrews 9 backs this up, talking about Christ being the High Priest who sacrificed himself *once* for all the people. Once for all.

But it also contains a time element. Once *for all time*. He only had to do it once. He didn't have to do it over and over again. The tenth chapter of Hebrews makes this very clear. The author of Hebrews says in verses 11 and 12 that if Christ didn't do it *once for all*, didn't do it in a complete manner, then he would have to keep doing it over and over again, and we know that's not happening. It was once *for all time*. He only had to do it once.

So Christ died to destroy sin and death. He only had to do it once, and he did it once for all people. So our lives should be characterized by being freed from sin because of what Christ has done. Not anything we do.

Remember back in the early chapters, Paul said you can't come to God on your own merits because they're worthless. It's what Christ has done for us.

In the same way, verse 11 states, "Count your lives dead to sin but alive to God in Christ Jesus." Dead to sin but alive to God. That means voluntary and intentional sin should no longer exist, because he said, "Do not let sin reign in your mortal body to obey its evil desires," (v. 15). "Do not offer the parts of your body to sin as instruments of wickedness."

In other words, don't volunteer to sin. Don't go into sin with your eyes open, knowing that you're sinning. It should not be a part of our lives anymore. You know when something is wrong. If you know something is not acceptable by God or if you know something will cause somebody else to sin, don't do it.

As James says in his book (4:17), if you know the right thing to do and you don't do it, you sin. Every sin comes with a choice or a chance to escape (1 Cor. 10:13). With every temptation to sin comes a way to escape. You will always have a choice, to sin or not to sin. Except, we know that in the lives of some people there are controlling sins that they can't seem to handle. Verse 14 answers that. "Sin shall not be your master, because you're not under law, but under grace."

In other words, if you are a truly born again Christian, truly starting over with a clean slate, there is nothing that should control your life except the Holy Spirit. That includes alcohol. That includes cigarettes. That includes any other thing that's out there. If those things are still controlling you, then you're not serving the right master. They can be conquered. It may not be instantaneous. It may not be immediate, but they can be conquered as you submit yourself to the leadership of God through the Holy Spirit.

So what is Paul saying in these verses? "Shall we go on

sinning so grace may abound; so God will continue to pour out his grace and mercy on us?" No, because God has been gracious to us to give us a chance to start over and sin should not be a part of our lives.

Now that sounds idealistic, and Paul knows it is idealistic. When we get to chapter 7, he will show us the other side of the coin. But as Christians, as people who have been set apart and been made holy and clean, sins that we are aware of in our lives need to be dealt with. One by one, day by day, they need to be put away or put behind us because they should not control us, and we should not willingly, voluntarily participate in them. That's because now we serve a higher power. Now we serve a God who is pure, holy, just, right and perfect. In order to please him we should be as near to perfect as we can be. We can do that neither in our own power nor in our own strength because that would be impossible. But we can be victorious in the power of Christ and the leadership of the Holy Spirit.

Has your tape been erased? Have you started over by the grace of God? If so, your new life should not be characterized by sin. Instead, you should be living a life patterned after Christ and by the help of the Holy Spirit learning to conquer sin.

CHAPTER 12

Now that I'm Free, What Do I Do?

Today's Bible Reading: Romans 6:15-23

Just as you used to offer the parts of your
body in slavery to impurity and to ever-
increasing wickedness, so now offer them in
slavery to righteousness leading to holiness.
Romans 6:19b

The Emancipation Proclamation signed by President Lincoln set many people free from their masters who held them in slavery up to the conclusion of the Civil War. Many of these freed slaves moved north and found work in factories that were being established at the beginning of the Industrial Revolution. Some became migrant farm workers moving from place to place to either plant or harvest crops as the seasons dictated.

But for many thousands of former slaves, who were primarily black people in a white society, the question they feared and for which there was no immediate answer was: "Thank God I'm free, but now what do I do? Where do I go from here?"

As Christians, Paul says we are faced with a very similar question spiritually. We have been set free from the bondage of sin because of what Christ did for us, but now what do we do? Should we continue to sin just because God is gracious, loving and forgiving? That's the question asked today and right up front Paul says, "By no means." That's not what we should be doing. We should not be getting ourselves involved again in the former way of life.

Remember the first question he asked back in verse 1 was "Should we go on sinning that grace may increase? By no means." He goes on and explains that because we have been given a new life the old life should be gone and done away with. We should be living a new life that is characterized by being saved from sin.

But now Paul asks, "Should we sin because we're not under law, but rather under grace?" Does the absence of the Law make a difference? As a matter of fact, no. He makes the point by saying, "You are in fact, in form or in theory a slave your whole life. Whether it is to sin, which characterized your old life, or to God; you are a voluntary slave. You are a slave to whatever or whomever you chose to be your master."

In Matthew 6:24 Jesus said you cannot serve two masters. You have to make a decision. When you decide to accept Jesus as your Lord your Savior you are saying, "I want You to take control of my life." The question we must then ask is did you really mean it? Did you really want Him to be your master or simply, your savior? Whom do you choose to serve? Is it sin or is it Christ? If you have been set free, it should be Christ. If you've been born again, it should be Christ.

You can't pretend to serve Christ and really serve sin. If you're really serving yourself by living in sin you really don't have Christ as your master. Since you have been reborn, you have made a choice of whom you wish to serve, at least in your head. Did you mean it in your heart?

Do you accept that gift of sanctification; being made free from sin, being made holy, being set apart from the world with its selfishness and its sinfulness; or do you want to continue as you used to?

Serving sin, selfishness and old habits is easy. It feels comfortable because that's what we know. It's what we're used to. It comes very easily to fall back on our natural instincts and our natural selves. But Paul says the outcome only leads to death, not only physically but also spiritually. If you continue to live in sin, if you continue to please yourself, if you continue to do things you know are wrong, the end result is simply death. Read verse 21 and the first part of verse 23.

> What benefit did you reap at that time from the things you are now ashamed of, for those things result in death...For the wages of sin is death.

Paul doesn't pull any punches. He makes it very plain, very clear, and very straightforward. If you continue to live to please yourself and live in sin—no matter what kind it is—the result is death.

But serving Christ and being obedient to the Word of God, is not so easy. It's not natural. Every hour of every day we are faced with decisions. What do I do? What should I say? Should I go there or shouldn't I?

We are faced with decisions time after time, moment after moment, and every single time we are faced with a decision we have to ask ourselves, what is right? What would Jesus do? What would God want me to do in this situation or as a response to these circumstances? It's uncommon. It's unnatural to be continually asking ourselves these things. It's more natural just to fall back on what we know and do things instinctively.

We can only live this righteous life by the power of the Holy Spirit, who Paul teaches in other places, comes upon us and wants to control us. We can only do it by submitting ourselves fully and completely to His leadership. When we do that what is the result?

"Now that you have been set free and have become slaves to God, the benefit you reap leads to holiness and the result is eternal life, for the gift of God is eternal life in Christ Jesus, our Lord," (v. 23).

Amen.

That is what's worth living for. That's worth the entire struggle, all the challenges, all the decisions we have to make day by day, knowing that the end result is eternal life.

You are a slave to whomever you chose to be a slave to. Do you want to continue to live in sin? Do you want to continue to please yourself? Do you want to continue to do the things that feel natural or do you want to serve the living God who has chosen to save you from that and give you a new life and a new start.

Slavery to sin is gone. Instead, we should be voluntary slaves to God.

In Matthew 12, Jesus again reminds us that if we don't let the Spirit of God come in and take control of us, then we're going to be worse off then than we were before.

Let's look at exactly what He says there. "When an evil spirit comes out of a man, it goes through places seeking rest and does not find it. Then it says, 'I will return to the house I left.' When it arrives it finds the house unoccupied, swept clean and put in order. This is the life that has been made clean from the evil spirit. This is the life that has been set free from sin. The spirit comes back and finds nothing in its place. Emptiness. The person has not let the Holy Spirit take control.

What does he do? "He goes and finds seven other spirits more wicked than him and they go in and live there. The result is the final condition of that man is that he is worse off than at the first. That's how it is with this evil generation," (Matthew 12:43-45).

Those people who claim to be set free from sin, claim to have Jesus as their Savor, yet continue to live in sin, find themselves in the same position as the man Jesus is talking about.

Peter declares the same thing in a different way in his second letter. He says this in chapter 2, starting with verse 20:

> If they have escaped the corruption of this world by knowing our Lord and Savior Jesus Christ, and then are again entangled in it and overcome they are worse off at the end then they were at the beginning. It would have been better for them not to have known the way of righteousness than to have known it and turned

their backs on the sacred command that was passed on to them. Of them the proverbs are true 'A dog returns to its vomit' and 'A sow that is washed goes back to her wallowing in the mud.'

Peter says, if you know the truth about Jesus Christ, that He is willing to save you in love, to reach out and accept you by faith, and you say, "Yes, I want that," but you continue to live in sin you are worse off than someone who has never heard, because you know the difference. You know Christ wants to set you free from those sins. He wants to set you free to live a life of righteousness, holiness and cleanliness, not one that is characterized by besetting sins and things that are displeasing to God.

The fact is, you are a slave to whomever you choose, whether it be to sin or to Christ. If you have taken Christ by faith, you have been set free from your sin, so you should voluntarily serve God.

The final fact that I would have you to know is if you have been truly born again by the saving grace of God and have made Him the Lord of your life, you will want to do all you can to please Him. You will not want to make Him ashamed of you.

Again I want to go back to the book of Matthew. Jesus teaches in chapter 7. He says,

> Not everyone who says to me "Lord, Lord" will enter the kingdom of heaven, but only those who do the will of my Father who is in heaven. Many will say to me on that day, "Lord, Lord did we not prophecy on your name and

> in your name drive out demons and perform
> many miracles?" Then I will tell them plainly, I
> never knew you. Away from me you evildoers!"
>
> Matthew 7:21-23

Get out of my sight. You were faking it the whole time.
I don't know you.

Are you faking it as you read this? Are you truly born
again? Do you have Christ, not only as your savior, but as your
lord? The one to whom you submit to as if you were a slave?

It sounds like a simple question, but it has a very
profound meaning. It's a difference between death and
eternal life.

I want to go way back to the Old Testament as I
close. It's a challenge God gave to the children of Israel. It
appropriately fits this lesson.

Some people continually ask the question, Isn't it too difficult
to live a life of holiness, to continually ask God for forgiveness, to
continually submit to God and live by His principles?

Here's what God says:

> Now what I am commanding you today is not
> too difficult for you or beyond your reach. It's
> not up in heaven so you have to ask, Who will
> go up there for me and bring it down? Nor is it
> beyond the sea so you will ask, Who will cross
> the sea for me and bring it back? The word is
> very near you. In fact, it's in your mouth and in
> your heart if you understand it. So you might
> obey it.
>
> See I set before you today life and prosperity
> and the opposite is death and destruction, for
> I command you today to love the Lord your

God, to walk in his ways and to keep his commands, decrees and laws, then you will live and increase. God will bless you...

But, if your heart turns away, and you're not obedient, and if you're drawn away to bow down to other gods and worship them, I declare to you this day that we will certainly be destroyed...This day I call heaven and earth as witnesses against you. That I have set before you life and death, blessings and curses. Now choose life, that you and our children may live and that you may love the Lord your God, listen to his voice, and hold fast to him.

Deuteronomy 30:11-16b, 17-18a, 19-20a

CHAPTER 13

Free to Serve

Today's Bible Reading: Romans 7:1-6

So, my brothers, you also died to the
law through the body of Christ, that
you might belong to another, to him
who was raised from the dead, in order
that we might bear fruit to God.
—Romans 7:4

Bumper stickers often make profound statements. Here's one that might have been seen back in the '70's: THERE OUGHT TO BE A LAW TO ABOLISH ALL LAWS. The concept behind such a statement was quite prevalent back then, that all established government was bad, so let's try to get rid of it. Fortunately, clearer heads prevailed and the government maintained its stability, or most of it, anyway because our country's leaders knew that any society functioning without laws is not really a functioning society. It's actually just plain chaos. It's a situation where everybody does, as the Bible says, "what is right in his own eyes." That makes no sense and is really no way to live. The people who toted slogans like that really wanted less government, not no government.

When we get set free from the legal code of the Old Testament law, we are not free to do just as we please. For if we were, we would not follow God. We would simply go back to living in sin.

We have instead been set free by the power of God for the purpose of serving God. That purpose is not intended to be mandatory. It is intended to be voluntary, willing and out of gratitude for what He has done for us.

In these verses Paul gives us another example of starting over. He says we are set free from the law to serve Christ. He starts by giving a comparison to a woman who is married and wants to be married a second time. Legally she cannot do that as long as her husband is still alive. That makes sense in most societies. Paul says that if the woman is married, she is bound by law to stay with her husband as long as he is alive. But once he is dead the marriage bond is broken. That's why when we have marriage ceremonies, we include the phrase in most services, "until God shall separate us by death" It is based on this verse and others in Scripture.

Marriage is legally binding until one spouse or the other dies or if the marriage is dissolved in some other fashion. But in Paul's discussion here he is using death as that severance point.

So he says for those who are bound by law to the Old Testament system the effect is the same. You are bound to that system unless the contract is broken. The covenant that bound you together is broken.

What did Jesus say at the Last Supper? He said, "This cup is the new covenant in my blood, which is poured out for you," (Luke 22:20). We understand from that and from other teachings that there is a new covenant in effect. We are not bound to live by the old covenant, the law.

So, just as long as your spouse is alive, you are bond to him/her. As long as the Law was in effect people were bound to it. But Christ says, "I have now done away with that. That is not your legally binding force anymore. Instead you are living by grace."

Living by grace is not intended to be a license to living in freedom either. Paul wants to talk about a comparison of what it is like to be living under the law and to be free from the law. First, let's look at what he says about living under the law. In verse 5 he says, "When we were controlled by the sinful nature, sinful passions aroused by the law were at work in our bodies." We were controlled by our sinful natures, he says. If we had lived under the Old Testament system we would have been controlled or our actions would have been subjected to the law which was then in force by the political leaders.

These laws, as we have mentioned a couple of times, were not intended to be what they actually were in practice, a list of criteria. Instead, they were intended to be reflections on society to show where we fall short of God's demands. When a person recognized when he fell short he could go to God for confession and forgiveness. It was supposed to act as a mirror, not a ruler.

On the subject of living under selfish desires, Paul gives a thorough discussion in the book of Galatians. In Galatians 5:19, he says, "Acts of the sinful nature are obvious." As we look around, we recognize things that are initiated and controlled by our sinful, selfish desires. He gives a list here, and we know some of these are true of ourselves or of people we know.

Sexual immorality. That's pretty rampant and obvious in our society. Impurity and debauchery. There is no need to comment on that. Idolatry and witchcraft. –They are false worship, in other words. People are not worshipping the true God even though they know the truth. Hatred. Discord. Jealousy. Fits of rage. Selfish ambition. There's one I have to be careful of. I've got more ambition than I know what to do with. Sometimes it's selfishly focused. Sometimes it isn't. I have to be careful. Dissentions or creating problems between people. Factions and envy. Boy, I wished there were churches that didn't have those things in them, but they do. Drunkenness, orgies and the like finish off the list.

This is a short list. We could add many more things to that list. Paul says this is what it's like to be controlled by your sinful nature. In other words, you live and do things that are pleasing to you, and you don't care what happens to anybody else. You don't care about the consequences that will follow later.

The law actually set up a standard of living or standard of behavior, as we know from the written record and by experience that was impossible to keep. There was a standard that was there, but it was so idealistic, no one could keep it. By recognizing that fact, we would know that we were sinful. We needed a Savior, we needed help, and we needed someone to rescue us from that condition. Then Christ comes along and he does away with that whole system and introduces us to a life of grace and love.

There are two reasons for the new birth that Paul talks about in these verses. Verse 4 reads, "So my brothers you also died to the law through the body of Christ. Why? That you might belong to another. That is to him who was raised from the dead." That's the first reason.

You were born again. You were renewed in your life. You had a new man introduced to you as a new nature for yourself. Because you now belong to Jesus, not to yourself. Under the old system you lived to please yourself; you lived to do things that were enjoyable without worrying about anybody else. Now, because you have been saved, because you have been renewed, because you've been given a new life, a new chance; you belong to the One who rescued you.

In 1 Corinthians 6:20, Paul says, "You are not your own. You were bought at a price."

When people buy a house, they will often buy it because they like the setting or the style of building. They buy it and sign the contract. A few days later they hire someone to come in and remodel the whole house. They do that because they like the house and its location, but they want the inside of the house set up to fit their own needs, desires or styles.

They might not like the kitchen cupboards on the left wall. They would prefer them on the right wall. Perhaps they want a different kind of flooring or whatever.

That house belongs to them. They can do what they want with it because they paid the price to purchase it.

Jesus paid the price for you and me. Now He wants to remodel us. He wants to change us. He wants to make us more like himself, more pleasing to himself instead of our former owner, sin.

The second reason he gives is that we might bear fruit

to God. Not only do we belong to God, but we should be producing something that is a blessing to God or a benefit to God.

Again we could go back to the Galatians 5 passage where Paul talks about the fruit of the Spirit.

What's it like to be living a life led by the Spirit? What characterizes that life? Paul lists a few things here. Love. You're concerned about the consequences of your actions and words, how it reflects on your neighbor and your friend. Joy. Because you know that you've been rescued and you know you have a future. Peace. Because you know you've been forgiven and you know that all things will work out for the good of those who love God. Patience, especially with those other people who are struggling with sin, these people who have not quite reached the point where you have, those people who may not always agree with you. You exercise patience because you know God loves them as well. Kindness, goodness and faithfulness both to God and to your fellow man. Gentleness and self control. These are all part of a Spirit-led life. Against such things there is no law and there cannot be.

We should be bearing fruit to God. That's one reason He wanted to rescue us. He wanted to change us. We should be producing things that are pleasing to God. Our lives should not only be living to please God, but as a consequence of our living in Jesus, other people are going to see and be influenced by our words or actions.

I'm sure that if we talked with a new believer, he would say it was the influence of some of his Christian friends that helped bring him to the Lord.

If you are a believer in Jesus Christ today, that is, if you have accepted Him as Savior and made him Lord of your life, you have been freed from the law. That freedom is not given to you to do as you please, but rather that you would commit yourself to serving the One who set you free. When you serve God willingly and wholeheartedly, other people will take notice and you will influence their lives as well.

God gives us a choice not unlike the challenge of Joshua of old. Choose you this day whom you will serve.

Will you choose to serve the living God who rescued you from sin or your selfish desires?

CHAPTER 14

Help! I'm Out of Control!

Today's Bible Reading: Romans 7:7-8:2

What a wretched man that I am! Who will
rescue me from this body of death? Thanks
be to God - through Christ our Lord!
—Romans 7:24, 25

I'm on a self-imposed diet. I got a report a little more than
a year ago that my cholesterol was a little high. The doctor
asked me to try to bring it under control. So I began to eat
differently. No more eating everything in sight, like I used
to do. I love to eat, but apparently food doesn't like my body
anymore, at least certain types. So I've chosen not to eat very
much red meat or dairy products. I've shifted over to more
fruits and vegetables.

Every once in a while temptation gets a little too strong.
Last night I had two cheeseburgers and some chips. That's a
big no-no for my diet. The result is that every time I break
the rule I have to work harder to offset what I have done. It

will take a few days to get those few elements of cholesterol I introduced last night out of my body again.

Paul says in these verses that we all have a similar problem spiritually. Since we have been redeemed by Christ and we belong to Him, we should know what is right and what is expected from us in order to keep fellowship with him. But every so often we fail. We give in. We commit a sin we know we shouldn't.

We have been sanctified by Christ. Paul tells us. By the blood of Jesus we have been set apart to be different from the people around us. No more living for self, but instead we should be living for Christ.

Yet, we find ourselves blending in with the crowd, don't we? We find ourselves being no different from our unsaved neighbors at times. When we get to the point where those sins, those trials, those tribulations, those temptations that come our way seem to overwhelm us, we want to cry out, "Help! I'm out of control! I need someone to rescue me."

Paul says (as he has told us two or there times already) the position of the law in that situation is helpless. First he asks, "Is the law itself sin because it is helpless?" No. The law is not sin in itself. When we think about the law as it was introduced in the Scriptures, it cannot be sin in itself, because God himself wrote the law and God never does anything that's bad. He would not give us or the Israelite people something that was sinful. It was, in fact, holy, righteous and good as Paul says in verse 12.

The law in itself was not sin. Its purpose was to point out how sinful we are, how far short we've fallen from the glory of God and from the requirements of God. It has done that well. Paul says, "I didn't even know what it meant to be covetous. I read the law and it says 'Do not covet.' So then, I started to investigate. What does it mean to covet? Well, it means to desire something you don't have, especially if it belongs to someone else. If the law had not told me that, I wouldn't have even thought about it. It wouldn't have been sin to me because I wouldn't have known that coveting was wrong." So the law pointed out sin. It exposed the sin of covetousness in Paul's life.

One of my professors at college used to describe it this way: If you as a parent have a young child and you don't want them to play in the street, you may go to the end of the driveway and draw a chalk line as a safety point. You tell the child not to go beyond the line for his/her own good. What's the child going to do? He's going to crowd the line. He's going to go over the line just to see what you will do. He's going to experiment with misbehavior. Now he knows it's a violation of a rule, which he might not have even thought about if you hadn't told him not to go there. The commandments (the Law) were there to expose our sinfulness.

Paul asks another question, "Well, if it was right and good at the beginning and it exposed my sinfulness, has its character changed?" (verse 13). Has what was good changed to something evil in order to condemn me; to put me to death? No. The character of the law has not changed at all, is Paul's answer. It has always been good, and it still is good. Its character has not changed. It's not something that changes like human character.

As we learn and as we grow, supposedly we develop in our character as well as physically. Hopefully our children are different now, if they are teenagers or older, than they were when they were younger, because they have learned from example as well as verbal teaching.

Paul says the law is not like a human being. It doesn't change. What it said back then is still true now. If it was good then, it's good now. It always was, and its purpose has not changed. The purpose was and is simply to point out how sinful we are.

So Paul says don't blame the law if you find sin at work in your life. It's not the law's fault. The law only points out your sin to you.

Then he goes on this wild grammatical tangle, you might call a verbal yarn ball. What in the world is he saying in verses 14-20.

In these verses, Paul says there is a spiritual battle going on inside each one of us. We have been set apart by Christ. That is, we have been sanctified by his blood, to be different from the world. We have started over. We have been born again and yet we often find ourselves acting just like everybody else. There is a spiritual battle going on inside each of us.

There are five things that need to be mentioned in relation to this. First of all, we know what the law, hence God or the Lord, demands of us. We read the Scriptures, both Old and New Testaments and we find basic commands and principles that we know God expects us to keep. Jesus said it was summed up in two statements. Love God and love your neighbor. Scripture actually goes beyond that and spells out many things for us. In Ephesians 4:7 Paul says if you actually learn to love your neighbor, forgive him or her, be ready to confess sins and to put things right when you know they are wrong.

We know from the Bible what God expects from us. That is our head knowledge. That is where our heart is placed in obedience to God. We want to do what we know is the right thing because we are the children of God. We want to please God. We want to do the right thing. We know we will be rewarded by God if we do that and we will avoid punishment or we will not lose some of the rewards that we were expecting.

Now, other people will know we are Christians by the way we conduct our lives. Do we live in obedience to God or to please ourselves?

Thirdly, we still find ourselves committing sins that we thought had already been gone; had already been done away with. We still face temptations and trials every day. So we might ask ourselves, what happened? I thought these things were gone. I thought I was set apart, made clean, started over. How come I am still struggling with sin?

Well, to be set apart by God does not make us immune from sin. If we were, then when we were born again we would become automatons. We would become robots. We would become instruments of God who could not violate His laws or principles. That's not what God wants. He wants loving obedience, willing obedience, in the face of trials and temptations.

So we find this war going on, Paul says. I want to do what I know is right and yet I find myself doing things I hate to do because I know they are wrong. What's going on? My sinful nature occasionally takes control. Occasionally I will succumb. I will give in. I will yield to temptation. I may say a bad thing about somebody. I may do something that I know is wrong because God has already pointed out to me before that he is not pleased with that thing. Yet, I find myself not helping myself. I find myself in the position where I just can't help it, and I give in. That's the sinful nature taking control again.

Paul says sometimes we get in that position. We know what we are supposed to do. We do what we know we're not supposed to do, and we ask ourselves, "What am I going to do? How am I going to get out of this mess? Some days I feel really close to God. Some days I feel great and wonderful, and everything is going well. Yet other days from the time I get up until I go to bed I face one temptation right after another. I fail. What is going on? Who is going to rescue me from this? How can I get out of this mess?

In our confession, in our temptation we can remember, by being reminded by the Holy Spirit that God is still in control and He can still be depended on. He can still rescue us from whatever situation we find ourselves in.

As Paul told the Corinthians in his first letter, there is no temptation given to us without a way of escape. We only need to come to God and beg his help. God has promised to keep us in his care until the day we see Him. Paul said in Philippians 1:6, "He has begun a good work in you and will be faithful to complete it." Just trust Him. Come to Him. Depend on Him. Recognize sin in your life or a temptation that you will be facing or are facing. Come to Him and ask Him, "Help. I need your strength."

Then rest assured that sin will not destroy you. It can only cause temporary damage. The first two verses of chapter 8 state, "There is now no condemnation to those who are in Christ Jesus." Yes, you are going to fail. Yes, you're going to slip into temptation and sin, but that doesn't mean you're condemned. It simply means you need help. It simply means that you slipped a little bit. There is no condemnation for you if you are truly in Christ.

In other places Paul says that when our faith is placed in Christ that is a guarantee for eternal life. That is a guarantee to receive an inheritance from God, an inheritance of eternal life.

Yes, we've been set apart. Yes, we should be different from the world. Yes, we are sanctified by His grace. Which all means we will not be condemned, but we still do face temptations.

Jesus did not displace the law because it was sinful or evil. He simply continued the working out of God's plan as it was introduced way back at the beginning. The law was never intended to save us from sin, but only point it out in our lives. Jesus's sacrifice introduced the period which we call the age of grace, where in we who are living today find ourselves. We can come freely to God and ask His help. We can ask Him for forgiveness, acceptance and cleansing.

We are saved, we are justified, we are sanctified all at once, but that isn't the end of it. Jesus's power is also with us every day to help us resist these temptations that we face, to help us to flee from sin, as Peter tells us to do, and to stand as a witness for Christ in our community.

Sometimes we're going to fail. Sometimes we're going to slip. Sometimes we're going to give in to temptations, but Jesus is right there beside us, ready to forgive us and welcome us back.

The law doesn't need to point out to me or you our shortcomings, because we know, inside ourselves we are sinful. We all need God's love. Sin doesn't need to control us anymore, because the power that is within us is greater than that which is in the world (1 John 4:4).

So when you feel out of control, when you feel that those sins, those temptations, those trials are becoming overwhelming to you, cry out to God. "Help! I'm out of control. Come and take control of my life. Thank you." I promise you He will.

CHAPTER 15

The Proof is in Your Practice

Today's Bible Reading: Romans 8:1-11

The mind of sinful man is death, but the
mind controlled by the Spirit is life and
peace; the sinful mind is hostile to God.
It does not submit to God's law, nor can
it do so. Those controlled by the sinful
nature cannot please God. You, however,
are controlled not by the sinful nature, but
by the Spirit, if the Spirit of God lives in
you. And if anyone does not have the Spirit
of Christ, he does not belong to Christ.
— Romans 8:6-9

James Bond is one of my favorite movie characters of all
time. I like James Bond movies. It's not because of the pretty
women that are in there, although they are attractive. and
it's not because of all the fast cars or planes or anything
like that. I like James Bond because he's able to operate
in all sorts of different situations and occasions changing

his identity. Sometimes he takes on different characters in different places in order to get the work done that he set out to do. As a viewer, I know who he is no matter where he is or what he is doing. I know he is James Bond, agent of the British government. I know he is actually impersonating somebody else when he is under certain circumstances. I know he's faking. Yet I accept him for what he is.

Paul tells us in the verses today that many people are trying to fake their way into the kingdom of God. It won't work. God is the one who sits back and sees everything that's going on. He knows who are his and who are not. Some people claim the lordship of Christ in their lives, but Paul says in these verses the proof is in how you live. The proof is in the practice.

He starts out by saying, "Therefore there is now no condemnation for those who are in Christ Jesus because through Christ the law of the Spirit of life has set me free from the spirit of sin and death," (verse 1).

You are no longer condemned to eternal punishment if you have been saved by the grace of God. He has said this several times, and he will probably say it several more before he is done.

Your sinful, natural, old self has been done away with. You have been born again. You've started over. You've got a new beginning. The old thing has been done away. There's a new you if you have been truly accepted by God.

God, himself, took the penalty. God, himself, took the punishment for you. Paul says in verse 3, "God fulfilled the requirements of the Law by sending his own Son in the likeness of sinful man to be a sin offering."

Now, in our country, we hear about people who have

been put on death row for some serious crime against society. The state in which they reside or in which the crime was committed has sentenced them to death. They wait, perhaps for years, for that sentence to be carried out. In the process through the legal maneuvering in our country, there comes a point when these people appeal to the governor of the state for a pardon. It's up to that governor to decide if that is a valid thing to do or not. If the governor, in his or her wisdom decides yes, this person has been in prison long enough, he's old, he's feeble and sickly, I will pardon him and let him go. That governor has now relieved that person of the penalty of death.

That's not what God has done. God is not the governor who pardons you. He is the person who steps in and accepts your full punishment. The governor of the state of Maine, New Hampshire or any other state will not go to the death chamber on behalf of a prisoner, because he can't. If he does, it's all over for him (or her). But God did that. God went to the death chamber *and came back* to fulfill the pardon, to help you escape the punishment that is yours because of your sin and mine as well.

Therefore there is no condemnation for you if you are in Christ Jesus. The sentence has been commuted, done away with because of what he did, by the grace of God.

But Paul doesn't leave it there. Those who are truly in Christ will live like it, he says. They will live accordingly. Starting with verse 5, he makes a comparison: those who allow sinful, natural habits to continue in their lives show that they are truly not letting God be the lord in their lives. "Those who live" he says in verse 5, "according to the sinful nature have their minds set on what their nature desires."

The mind of the sinful man is death (v. 6). Verse 7 states, "The sinful mind is hostile to God, it does not submit to God's law, nor can it do so."

Is this the picture of a Christian? No. Is this the picture of somebody who's following God? No. It's that person who never fully submitted to God. The old sinful nature is still in control. It has not been put away! But those who are living in accordance to the Spirit of God have their minds set on what the Spirit desires. They acknowledge, they long, and they desire to please God in everything they do.

Who is in control? Paul asked in the previous chapter. Is it sin or is it God? Who is truly in control, Satan or the Spirit of God? And he says that is revealed by how you live. Because what you do, where you go, and what you say reveals your true character.

I have a terrible tendency to sin. I was tempted this week many times. One or two times I remember hearing some juicy gossip or I witnessed a certain event. I would tell myself, I just can't wait to tell somebody. Next time I see that person I'm going to tell her what I just discovered about somebody else. Then the Spirit would say, would that be really helping that person or would you be putting them down? Then I'd start an argument. I'm only telling the facts. But are the facts helpful in this case? They don't hurt. Who's in control, you or Me?

We have to be careful; we will struggle with this kind of thing constantly. Paul told us that back in chapter 7. Who is in control, is it the Spirit of God or is it my sinful nature? How we act reveals who is in control. Those who allow the Spirit of God to have control will act more and more like Christ each day. Peter said in one of his letters we should be growing in the likeness of Christ; progressively growing more and more toward perfection.

Recently, in Christian circles, and somewhat in larger circles, WWJD was spreading all over the place. What Would Jesus Do? It became a glib question, but it shouldn't. It should be a serious question for each one of us, an honest question for us. In every situation, what *would* Jesus do if he were here? What would Jesus say in response to that person, that question or that accusation? That should be an honest question we ask constantly if we want the Spirit to control us. People who are controlled by the Spirit, Paul says in the Ephesians letter (Chapter 4) would be quick to forgive, slow to anger, ready to accept other people for who they are in the church of God. Other people's opinions and ideas that do not contradict biblical teachings or principles, we should not argue or debate. We shouldn't get into a huff and ready to defend our point of view if theirs is equally valid.

Again, Paul said to Timothy, don't get caught up in petty arguments. They only lead to quarrels and dissentions which are displeasing to God (1 Timothy 6:3-5).

Paul is telling us in these verses those who live according to the sinful nature do not have their minds on God. Their mind is on themselves, there mind is on the cravings that they have whether it be for drugs, sex, alcohol, spreading gossip, or whatever it is. That's where their mind is. It's not on God. But the person who is led by the Spirit is constantly asking himself, what am I doing to please God? What else can I do to please God? Your life will reveal who is truly your master.

Paul says one more thing in verses 10 and 11. "But if Christ is in you, your body is dead because of sin, yet your

Spirit is alive because of righteousness." Your spirit is alive because of what God has done for you and in you and through you. "And if the Spirit of him who raised Jesus from the dead is living in you, He who raised Christ from the dead will also give life to your mortal bodies through his Spirit, who lives in you." In other words, who is in control of your life determines your destiny. Is the sinful nature going to lead you anywhere but to destruction? No. Is Satan going to lead you anywhere but to destruction? No. Can you lead yourself anywhere but to destruction? Again, No. Therefore, why not let the Spirit who gives you immortality lead you. He gives you eternal life, if you let him be your Lord.

The proof that Jesus is your Lord is discovered by the way you live. Are you living like there was no tomorrow or are you living with an eternal hope that nothing can take away?

CHAPTER 16

Adopted by the King

Today's Bible Reading: Romans 8:12-17

> For you did not receive a spirit that makes
> you a slave again to fear; but you received
> the Spirit of sonship. And by him we cry,
> 'Abba, Father.' The Spirit himself testifies
> with our spirit that we are God's children
> —Romans 8:15, 16

On one occasion in our church we had three boxes in which to collect small gifts for some of our young people. When they received these, each one received one large package, but inside the larger package there were several smaller ones. They didn't know what was in any of them until they opened them. They were surprised and happy to receive those gifts.

One large gift with several smaller ones inside it is what Paul is talking about as we have already found out in early parts of the book of Romans. That's what we receive when we accept Christ as our Savior. We have found already that when we exercise our faith we receive salvation from eternal destruction. Along with that we have already discovered and talked about justification that is a gift that comes along with salvation. That means we are not guilty before God, the judge, because of what Christ has done for us. A second gift is attached to the first.

But there is another one we had begun to talk about—sanctification. That's being set apart. We accept Christ into our lives. He not only saves us and purges us from our past sins, but He sets us apart to Himself to be special, different, or in theological terms, we are holy. Unlike the rest of the world, we are consecrated to God and to His service.

Now, inside that package of sanctification there are smaller packages. We've seen that one of them is the power to overcome sin in our lives. That's what all of chapter 7 was about, the struggle with sin and relying on Christ for that victory. The gift of overcoming power comes with sanctification. That power comes with being set apart, being different. People of the world don't have the same kind of struggle. They give in to the control of sin. We don't (or we shouldn't), and we can rely on Christ for the victory.

In today's text (verses 12-17), we find that we have been adopted by the King of Kings, the Lord of Lords, the Creator of all. What a wonderful blessing that is. Paul tells us this adoption is part of the work of the Holy Spirit. It is the Spirit of Him who raised Jesus from the dead that gives us hope, he says in verse 11. Part of the work of the Holy Spirit (He has multiple responsibilities) is to make us understand that we are truly members of God's family. We have been adopted.

Now why does Paul use the term adopted? Simply

because of what Adam did (as Paul describes in the early part of this book, chapter 3 especially) we have been separated from God by sin. We are not part of his family. We are not part of his world, really, except physically. And so Paul describes to us, in these terms, that Christ, in his love, reached to us who are strangers to God because of sin and said, "I love you and want to adopt you."

That's what a lot of families do to children who have been abandoned or somehow lost their parents, right? They have a real love in their heart for a particular child, so they reach out to that child and say, "I love you. I want to adopt you. We want you to be a real part of our family." That's love.

That's what Christ has done for us. We were not part of his family, but we can be through this adoption that he offers us.

It is a popular misconception promoted by many different groups, people who don't understand the truth of Scripture, that everybody is a child of God. That concept has been and will probably always be circulated, but it is false. If it were true, we would not be given an opportunity to become children of God, because we already would be. In John 1:12, what does the writer there tell us? "But as many as received Him to them He gave the power to become the children of God through faith" (through believing). Now, if we already were children of God we would not need to be adopted. We would not need to come into God's family. An offering of adoption assumes we are not a part of the family yet. That teaching that everybody is a child of God is not biblical.

We need to become children of God, and we do become

children of God as a part of the large package, a gift given us through the Holy Spirit.

Paul says in verse 12 as children of God we have an obligation. Therefore, since God has adopted us, we have an obligation, but it's not to our old sinful nature anymore. That's gone. That's over. That's behind us. It's not an obligation or an attempt to repay any sort of debt for what Christ has done for us. We can't do that. If we tried to pay God back for what Jesus did on the cross it would not longer be a gift.

If somebody gave me a gift, for a birthday or Christmas, and I calculated the value of that gift and determined approximately what they paid for it, would it be right for me to go to that person and say, "I'll give you the value of that gift to thank you for it?" No. It would no longer be a gift if I did that. The point of giving a gift would be lost. You don't pay back someone who gives you a gift. You accept it graciously. You accept it with the intent that it was given out of love, friendship, fellowship, or some other reason. Neither can we pay God back for what He has done for us. There's no way we could match the value of the sacrifice of Jesus.

So we're not obligated to the old sinful nature. That's gone. We're not obligated to pay God back for what He has given to us. Our obligation, then, lies in our relationship. As children of God, we have an obligation to obey God just as a child growing up has an obligation to obey his or her parents.

In Exodus 20:12, one of the Ten Commandments, Moses writes, "Children, obey your parents." But the sentence didn't stop there. "Children, obey our parents so that it may go well with you in the future." You see, obedience to our parents is for our own good. Our parents, being older, wiser people, know what's best for us in most cases, and they direct our lives in ways in which they would like to see us go. As children, if we are obedient to our parents, we're doing it because we know they know what's best for us and it's for our own benefit.

Our relationship to God is very similar. We need to obey God and all that He asks us to do, because we know God wants the best for us. We know He won't misdirect us. We know He will guide us well and good.

Jesus said, "Even as a father knows what's best for his children, how much more God knows what's best for His children" (Matthew 7:9-11).

We need simply to obey God, because as adopted children the same level of commitment is required of us as that of a child to his natural or biological parent.

Now when we say that God has the best in mind for us, we don't always receive immediate physical blessings in this life. We all know we have troubles, we have trials, and we have setbacks. We are told in other places of Scripture those come along by the hand of God on purpose, for our own growth spiritually, physically and socially.

But there are blessings that Paul mentions in these verses that we can receive or we can count on because we are children of God.

Verse 17 states, "If we are children, then we are heirs—heirs of God and co-heirs with Christ, if indeed we share in his sufferings, in order that we may also share in his glory." It's a short statement with a big, big message.

We can't really describe the love of God. We don't even know, and even if we knew we couldn't describe all we stand to inherit from God. It's such a wonderful, indescribable blessing.

Now if we think of God in his true character, being the God of the universe, being the God who created everything, being the God who is over and above all and everything is under His control, and we stand to inherit that, can you imagine?

If someone dies in this world and leaves a million dollars or two to somebody, that's a wonderful thing to the one who inherits that, but that's temporary. It may be gone in a few days or weeks.

What God offers us is permanent and eternal. He offers us a chance to inherit eternal life.

Now, let's think about that just for a second. When someone in this world inherits something, the person he inherits it from has to die. He or she has to pass on and leave it to them. That's what an inheritance is.

Our God has already promised us that we are heirs of all that He says, but He won't die. Correction. He has already died. He has already gone once, but He came back again to prove he was victorious, to prove He was all-powerful, to prove that He was in fact, the God of all. Because He died, it validates the inheritance.

We get eternal life as one of the things we inherit. We can live forever in His presence. We can live forever with this God who loves us so much as his adopted children.1 John 5:11 and 12 tells us that we get this eternal life as soon as we accept Christ. "This is the testimony: God has given us, eternal life and this life is in His Son. He who has the Son has life and He who does not have the Son does not have that life." In Ephesians 1:14 we are told the Holy Spirit that comes in when we receive Christ guarantees that inheritance for us. So, we have eternal life already, it has already begun. It will never end for us.

In John 14, what did Jesus promise us? In verses 2-4 he says, "I go to prepare a place for you and if I go I will come again and receive you unto myself." We are guaranteed a home in glory, a home in the presence of Almighty God. In celebration with all the angels and all those who are going with us, we will be there with God and with Christ our Savior.

We have been adopted by the King! We are part of his family, and we stand to inherit wonderful blessings. There's another topic we will talk about later.

If you have accepted God's plan of salvation, all that we have talked about in this lesson is yours. You have been declared "not guilty." You have been separated from sin to Christ. You have been adopted by the King of the universe, the King of Kings and Lord of Lords, and you have a wonderful future ahead of you.

If you have done all that, go and be obedient children.

If you haven't done that yet, I pray that you will do that, you will rejoice with us, you will stand with us, and you will live with us in the presence of God forever.

CHAPTER 17

Meanwhile, Back on Earth

Today's Bible Reading: Romans 8:18-30

I consider that our present sufferings
are not worth comparing with the
glory that will be revealed in us.
—Romans 8:18

Did you hear the one about the three hunters and the honey tree? It seems that they had been out hunting all day but had no luck finding any deer. While they were walking out along an old logging road they came upon a tree that was buzzing with bees. They checked it out and discovered a huge cache of honey.

"How are we going to get this honey home?" one of them asked.

"Well, we don't have anything to put it in," said another. "We'll have to mark the tree and come back later to get the honey."

The third one was a little suspicious of the other two because he lived a little distance away and thought perhaps they might get the honey. So he spoke up and said, "I'll tell you what. You two stay here. I'll run home and get some clean buckets. When I come back we can put the honey in the buckets."

So he left.

An hour went by. Two hours. Finally, one of the two left behind said, "I don't think he's coming back. Have we got anything we can put honey in?"

So they scrounged around and found some plastic bags or whatever else they had in their backpacks. So they decided they would take some of the honey.

Just as they were about to dig into that tree a voice comes out of the forest saying, "You touch that tree, I'm not going to get any buckets!"

They had a hope for something nice. Somebody let them down.

Now Paul has already told us that we have a great future in store for us. He talked about our relationship with God and he talked about our future with God. He says in verse 18,

> I consider that what we're going through right now, as wonderful as that seems, with all the blessings of God that we get in this life, that's nothing compared to what's ahead of us. That's nothing compared to what God has in store for us. We're going to be set free from this physical world and we're going to be in the presence of God Almighty.

All of creation, he says, is groaning, waiting patiently for the day when God is going to set us free and create a new world. There won't be any of the terrible things we face now in it. There will be no more pain, no more suffering, no more crying, no death or any of those things.

We read in the book of Revelation, in the 21st chapter where John describes his vision of the New Jerusalem. Travel with me, if you will. We are floating through space, and we come to this big ball we see in front of us. It slowly develops into something with a clearer image. We see a road of pure gold, sparkling like the sun. As we follow it, we come to this wall made up of pure, bright, gleaming crystals of various colors. Inset into these walls are huge pearls which represent the doorways or gates.

We approach one of the pearls, and it swings open with an angel standing there tending the door for us. We walk through on streets of shining gold, down the middle of which runs a river, and on either side are rows of fruit trees in full bloom with full, fresh fruit on them along with fruit that is half-grown. The description given is that they will continually produce fruit. Provision from God.

As we follow the road further, on either side, are huge, glorious places for people to dwell. Millions of people have joined us on the road by now, and we are drawn to the center where there is a bright glow that as you approach you recognize is the throne of God. You realize that you have made it. You are in the presence of Almighty God, fully and completely.

That's what lies ahead of us, Paul says. That is what's waiting for us once we've been adopted, once we've been accepted, once we've been a part of the family of God.

But meanwhile back on earth where we are now, we have to go through this life. We have to finish this life. That means we have to struggle with all the things we are facing.

This world is full of disappointment, defeat and death. We have to face all those things on a daily basis. It's a world of disappointment because not everything goes the way we want it to go, does it? From the time you got up this morning until now you've probably had some minor disappointments. Something didn't go right. Something didn't turn out right. Somebody disagreed with you. Those are the disappointments we face.

Only this week a young man shared with me that he had a major disappointment in his life. We face those things as we go through life. There are things that don't go our way.

Sociologists tell us that the present age in which we are living has the highest rate of depression on record. Why is that? It is because people can't face disappointment. They can't face being let down, because they don't have somebody or something to trust in.

We face disappointments every day, and for those people who can't face it or can't handle it, that represents defeat. We face a world of defeat because our plans fail or they get foiled, messed up. We may have career goals, family goals or financial goals and they fall through. We think we're defeated.

People fail us from time to time. We depend on somebody to get a job done, and when we ask them about it, they say, "No, I didn't get to it." Deadlines are set. They come and go, and the jobs are not done. People are disappointed. People are let down. We know that people fail us in many areas of life.

We know, too, that in our personal lives our health fails from time to time. All of us know what it's like to be sick in one way or another. Some of us face serious, tragic illnesses. Others are fortunate to be afflicted with minor ones. But health is not guaranteed. It is not perfect in any of us. As we grow older, we realize that more and more.

So we face a world of disappointment. We face a world of defeat. But we also face a world of death.

As we look around us, we know that in nature everything passes. Everything that's alive eventually dies, whether it is an insect that lives only for a few hours or a tree that lives for many years. Eventually it dies. That is a part of nature. That's the way God designed it, because the old things must pass away to make room for the new.

Every person who has been born faces death. We all face death. We know it's a part of our existence. We suffer the death of friends, family, and other loved ones. We must face it. We must realize that death is real and something we have to live with.

Moses at one time prayed a lengthy prayer to God. It was not all of praise, although he starts it out that way. But he recounts to God some of the things he was thankful for and some of the things that he had gone through, and he mentions death in that prayer (or the finality of life). He says in Psalm 90 verses 9 and 10, "We finish our years with a moan. The length of our days is seventy years or eighty, if we have the strength. Yet their span is but trouble and sorrow. For they quickly pass and we fly away."

Moses got the concept. He understood that life is brief. We all have to end it sometime. He also understood that going through life is not easy. We face tragedies and trials every day.

Thank God we do have someone we can depend on. We have someone who will help us.

Paul continues to say from verse 26 on, that the Spirit of God is there to help us in our struggles. We don't have to face the world alone. In fact, if we tried we would become severely depressed as many people are without God.

First he says, in relation to the Spirit, that we don't always understand how we should pray or what we ought to pray for. Sometimes we don't realize exactly how to pray or we struggle with prayer. There are three reasons for that. One, we don't know the mind of God. Two, we don't know the will of God. Three, we can't always explain our feelings.

We don't know the mind of God because He is perfect. He is all-knowing, and his plan has been set down and put into motion from before the time the earth was even created. We simply need to read Scripture, listen to the voice of God and try, by the influence of the Holy Spirit, to understand what our part in the whole plan is. He will help us do that, but since we don't know the mind of God sometimes it is difficult to know what to pray for.

Does God want us to move out in a certain direction in ministry or not? We don't know. That makes it difficult to pray because how can we pray accurately if we're not sure what God wants us to do?

We don't know what the will of God is in many areas. We kind of have to test the waters a little bit. We pray that God, through his Spirit, will direct us through the testing, through the trials and errors. That's how we can find out what we're good at, what we're not good at, where the open doors are, and when they are closed.

We don't know what to pray for or how to pray. Sometimes, I find, and I know some of you have experienced this, that when you come before God you are full of emotion. You want to be committed to your Lord and your Savior and when you approach Him you are there, but you don't know how to say what's on your mind.

Or maybe you are going through a very tragic time in your life. Someone close to you has passed away or a family has broken up. You come before God, and all you can say is, "Lord, I don't know what to say, but I know you are there, and I just want you to listen to me. Just try to figure out for me what's going on. Try to get me through this."

Emotions play a big part, because we are emotional people. Since we don't know exactly what the mind of God is, what the will of God is, and since we don't know exactly how to express our hopes, our desires, and our feelings; the Spirit is there to translate all of those things jumbled up inside us to God the Father so he'll hear us and understand us. So he'll know what we're praying for.

The Spirit also is there to remind us that everything is going to be all right. Verse 28 is a verse that many people quote, especially in times of difficulty, but it's good and appropriate at any time. "And we know that all things work together for the good of those who are in Christ Jesus."

All things work together. In other words, if you look at the larger picture, everything will be all right. You might be going through a trial right now; you might be suffering a setback right now, but everything will be all right.

God knows everything and He has already promised

us a wonderful future. He has already promised us that he will "never leave us or forsake us" (Hebrews 13:5). That's hope. That's an encouraging statement. That will help see us through, by helping us see the bigger picture.

We are also reminded that God knows the heart of everyone. He knows who are really his and who are not. He knows if you really mean business when you say you want to live for Christ or not.

Paul says, "I consider that what we are going through worth comparing with what we will have in the future." We have a wonderful life if we trust God, if we live for God, if we walk hand in hand with God in spite of its challenges; but friend, it's nothing compared to what's waiting for us.

I hope, right now, that you put your trust in Christ. I pray that you're looking forward to walking those streets of gold with me. If not, you are struggling through life on your own, finding it very difficult. I know you are. But you don't have to.

God is there. He wants to help you. Let the Spirit be your guide.

CHAPTER 18

Now That's Security!

Today's Bible Reading: Romans 8:31-39

For I am convinced that neither death
nor life, neither angels nor demons,
neither the present nor the future, nor
any powers, neither height nor depth,
nor anything else in all creation, will
be able to separate us from the love of
God that is in Christ Jesus our Lord.
—Romans 8:38, 39

I heard a woman call into a radio talk show to talk to
Governor Angus King of Maine who was a guest on the
show. She asked him if he or anyone else could put in writing
a guarantee that the power would not go out on January 1,
2000. Of course Governor King said, "I can't make that
kind of guarantee. We've done everything humanly possible
to prevent it, but there are some things beyond human
control."

What is there in our life that is absolutely guaranteed? When you buy any manufactured item on the market, most of them come with a warranty of sorts. It may be short or it may be rather lengthy, but that warranty gives you a sense of assurance that the product will be free from defects and will last for a period of time. But eventually the warranty runs out, right? Usually the product fails shortly afterward.

What is there in our life that is guaranteed? Think about our country for a minute. Next to a few in Western Europe or perhaps Egypt, ours is currently one of the longest standing governments in the world. What guarantee do we have that it will be here in another generation or two from now?

Is there anything in our world that is absolutely guaranteed? Not if you look at those kinds of things.

When we come to this place in Paul's letter, he is asking us to reflect on all that he has talked about up to now. To get a detailed look you would have to go back and reread the letter up to this point. Basically Paul has told us there is no excuse not to know God. There is no excuse not to embrace God, and when we do embrace God there are mighty and wonderful blessings waiting for us. When we unwrapped that package one wrapper at a time up to this point, we found that God gives us salvation, God gives us justification, God gives us sanctification, and along with those things comes adoption into God's family and a future with God in heaven. All of those things are ours by faith, not by works and not by the law.

So Paul says, "When you consider everything I've said up to this point, what can we say in response to this?" What can we say about all this? If God is for us and He's provided all these things for us and we just have to reach out and take it, who can deny it to us? Who can take it away from us? "Who," he says, "can be against us?"

If God did not spare his own Son, but gave him up for us on the cross, sacrificing him on our behalf; if he is the one who has justified us and says we're not guilty, who can condemn us? Who can take away that gift from us? Can anybody at all?

We've been set apart from the wicked world, consecrated unto a holy God. We've been adopted by the King of Kings and Lord of Lords. We've been guaranteed an inheritance in his presence forever and ever. Is there anyone or anything that can take that away from us? Paulsays, "Let's think about that."

First, let's think about the who. Who can separate us from the love of Christ? Anybody you know? Can your family members take away your love for God? Can your friends separate you from God? Think about your acquaintances or coworkers; can any of these people take away your love of God? No. They cannot step between you and God because your relationship between you and God does not involve any other people.   What about any government or agency (referred to in Scripture as powers and principalities)? Can any of those separate us or take away our relationship with God? No. You cannot outlaw a relationship with God. You can outlaw (and people have tried) forms of worship, places of worship and other modes and activities involved; but they cannot take away your relationship with God.

Consider what has happened in countries where they have tried to eliminate Christianity. What has it done?

In the first church we read about in Scripture, the more they were oppressed, the faster it spread. We know from more recent history that when the church is outlawed and is tried to be put down, it spreads. The effort backfires. No one can separate you from the love of Christ by law or by government.

Can any social or economic force such as a fad or a trend separate you from God? If it becomes popular to ignore God and go your own way, will that separate you from God because everybody else is? No.

In our recent history under the administration of Jimmy Carter we saw a trend where everybody jumped on the bandwagon and claimed to be born again, right? Although for many of them their interpretation of what that phrase meant was a far cry from the biblical meaning. Did they dilute our relationship with God for those of us who are truly born again? Those who are truly children of God? Did it change that relationship? No. Many people got a false impression of what it meant, but it did not take away what was real because it can't come between us and God.

Can anybody become too rich, too wealthy? Can anyone become so wealthy that they would lose their relationship with God? Consider Abraham. Consider Job. Consider Boaz. All three were wealthy men. Did that impede their relationship with God? No.

What about the reverse? Can anybody be so poor that it would deprive them of a relationship with God and a strong faith in God? No. You could be the most destitute person in the world, but if you have the love of God in your heart and a close relationship with Him, you are one of the richest. You are wealthy.

What about being famous or not so famous? Can your fame come between you and God? Not if you are faithful to Him, and He allows that fame to occur. We think of people like Louis Palau, Billy Graham, or other players in the Christian world whose names are known the world over. Their relationships with God were not affected by their fame.

On the other hand, some people who are isolated from the world (they may be in prison, nursing homes or confined to their own homes) who are truly born again, truly children of God, they've got it all. They are not prisoners. They are just as important, just as wealthy, as well off, as the people who are in the public eye.

What about on the spiritual side of things? Can any religion, group, or ideology change our relationship with God? Not if that relationship is real. No religious leader, no matter how charismatic he might be, can change what God has given to us or take it away. If we have received the gift and opened it, it is ours to keep.

Somebody may come on the scene and persuade the whole world to follow after him because he has the right way, the right truth. But if it is not biblical truth, it's wrong.

If we have the biblical truth in our hearts and we have embraced Christ and recognize the wrong that such a person is teaching, even though we may stand apart from the rest of the world, we've got it all. We're right. We have embraced the true and living God against whom no one can stand.

What about the local church or any small religious group or organization? Can they dictate what you believe and how you should worship? Some try. Some succeed to some degree, but if you have a true and close relationship with God, worship will come from your heart and will be expressed in ways that are personal to you, whether it happens at home or in public.

What about circumstances such as natural disasters, illness or death or anything else that may come into our lives? What about changes in our lifestyles that occur for one reason or another? Can any of these take away our love of God or God's love for us? No. More often than not they strengthen our bond. We have seen time after time in our country recently when tragedies occurred and people's faith was strengthened. People are killed. Storms come and go. Disasters happen. Through it all we hear people praising God, thanking God, and giving Him the credit. Faith is actually strengthened, not diminished.

"Who shall separate us from the love of Christ?" Paul asks. The answer is no one or no thing. You could make your own list of things that could challenge your faith yet through all those things we are more than conquerors through Him who gives us the strength, through him who loves us.

In verse 39, near the end, Paul says, "I am convinced that nothing else in all creation will be able to separate us from the love of God that is found in Christ Jesus." When you think about that statement, that really says it all. If there is nothing in all of creation that can separate us from the love of God, we have to stop to think of what is included. There is nothing that exists outside God himself that He did not create. Everything else is created.

God the Father, God the Son and God the Spirit are one unit. They are the God-head. Everything else is created including the physical world and the spiritual world. The angels, the demons, all those spirit forces were created. If nothing in all of creation can separate us from the love of God, it includes everything out there, except God himself.

God doesn't want to separate us from himself. He wants to draw us to himself.

So, if we consider that as fact, that there is nothing that exists which can separate us from the love of God, then we should have confidence in God. For He said, "I will receive you unto myself." He said, "I give you a guaranteed inheritance." He said, "No one can take you out of my hand." That is confidence. That is someone we can depend on. That is something we can live by day after day. To paraphrase, Peter said from one of his letters, "knowing this should make us the most joyous people on earth." It will give us the joy unspeakable and full of glory. (1 Peter 1:8)

How much more confidence do you need? God is there, He is there because He's the only one that has never been created. He has existed from eternity past. Everything else has been created, and there's nothing within creation that can separate us from Him. It's a guaranteed thing. What more do you need?

Paul says that is security. That is something you can put your confidence in if you have truly received Christ as your Savior. There's no one or nothing that can change that. It's permanent.

Hallelujah.

CHAPTER 19

Lord, Save My Family

Today's Bible Reading: Romans 9:1-29

It [salvation] does not, therefore, depend on
man's desire or effort, but on God's mercy."
—Romans 9:16

Suppose a woman who was interested in genealogy discovered
an old will left by an ancestor in her family. In the will was
a statement which said a large sum of money would be left
in a fund for scholarships for anyone who could prove he/
she was a direct descendant of this benefactor.

Upon checking at the bank named in the will, she finds
out that it is true. The money had been there for quite some
time, and no one had taken advantage of it. In the interval
it had grown to quite a large sum. Immediately the woman
notified everyone in her family who had children, so they
might take advantage of this opportunity.

Some were glad and excited, immediately applying for
some of the funds. Others hesitated. They wanted to find

our more about this to know for sure that they qualified. They waited a while hoping to gain more information. Still others chose not to believe her. They thought, *Nothing is free in this life. There's a catch somewhere.* So they missed out.

Now she is faced with a decision. Leave it like that, notify them once and let them decide or continue to remind the obstinate members of her family of what they are missing out on?

She has found something wonderful that her family could benefit from. What is she to do with those who don't want it?

Paul finds himself in a very similar situation as we open up chapter 9. Remember what happened at the end of Chapter 8? Paul has gotten so excited about all that God gives us as Christians. He has gotten really excited, really built up, and he's trying to remind us of what we get: eternal life, eternal security, a home in heaven, a close relationship with God and all the things that are waiting for us in the future. Then he opens up chapter 9 and says, "I wish all my brother and sister Jews could take part in this, but they haven't and it breaks my heart." "My heart is broken," Paul says, because these people, who have in the past been God's chosen people, have refused to take advantage of the free gift that has been offered to them.

What Paul is saying in the general concept here is that historically speaking, Jews have had a special privilege because from the time of Abraham, God has chosen one family and all his descendants to be his special people and through them he made many revelations of himself and promises to the whole world that would take place through him. Israel has not accepted salvation through Christ, and therefore she has rejected all the wonderful things discussed in chapter 8.

Many people we know have grown up in church, have knowledge of God, understand the Scriptures and yet reject the Christ. What a wonderful blessing they are missing out on. They know the plan of salvation, but they don't accept it for themselves. That should cause us to have great sorrow and increasing anguish like Paul had. These people around us are our friends and our family members. We should be like Paul and become so upset because they are not in the family of God.

Paul doesn't just stop right there and leave it at that. He wants to remind us we should not blame God for the situation. It's not God's fault. The fault lies with the people who have rejected Him.

The Israelite people were God's special people by the covenant he made with Moses, Abraham and Isaac. But they were not faithful.

He tells us again in a complicated way in verses 6-9, the true Israelites, the true children of God, the Jews are not those who can claim family heritage from Abraham necessarily. There were millions of those people, but not many were saved. The true Israelite, in Paul's view, is one who can claim God as his Father through faith. He discusses that back in chapter 4 where he talks about Abraham as being the father of faith and those who have accepted Christ by faith can claim Abraham as their true father because that promise came through him.

But he expands it at the end of the series of verses to say that that is also true of the Gentiles. We don't become Israelites, but we do become children of God. We do become part of God's family. In that sense, that very general sense, you can say we become descendants of Abraham and Abraham is the father of our faith.

Just because the plan of salvation is put out there and just because it is explained well, thoroughly and often, does not mean everyone will be saved, unfortunately. Not everyone will be. God desires it were true (2 Peter 3:9), but in fact, that it is not so. Not everyone will be saved.

That is what Paul is saying in verses 10-18 about Esau, Jacob, and Pharaoh. A lot of people misread that to think that God decided beforehand who was going to be saved and who wouldn't. That's not what Paul is saying. Paul is not saying that God chose before the beginning of the world who would be saved and who wouldn't, but, in fact, he knew who would accept him and who would reject him. There's a difference.

Paul is saying that God knew in his omniscience those who would refuse him, those who would reject him and those who would choose to follow him. If it were true that people who were good and right and raised in good families would become children of God that would rule out Jacob. Jacob was a scoundrel from the time he was young, and his behavior was anything but honest many times. Yet he chose to follow God, and God accepted him by faith.

It would also rule out many people in our lives whom we know in our time who are not perfect. God does not accept us by our works. He accepts us by our faith. There's a difference.

Paul also makes the point that those who reject God are not necessarily rejected by God completely. Remember, he is putting this in a historical time frame. We know he chose

Moses to lead Israel. That was on the positive side. Pharaoh refused to give in to what God said. He brought Moses and Aaron to preach to Pharaoh saying "let my people go!" Pharaoh refused. Because Pharaoh rejected God, God used him and his own plan in the deliverance of Israel. It was Pharaoh's resistance, Pharaoh's rejection, that in fact, showed the power of God. If Pharaoh had not hardened his heart there would not have been the ten plaques. If he had not resisted God's will the Israelites would not have seen how powerful God was before they trusted him in their journey through the wilderness. They would not have known God was strong enough, powerful enough and ready to carry them into the unknown, which was where they were going.

God used Pharaoh to strengthen the faith of the Israelites. He uses unbelievers often to strengthen our faith, by challenging us, by resisting us and by opposing us. What will we do? Will we learn to depend more heavily on God or will we give in and yield to the pressures around us?

In verses 19-21, Paul reminds us that God has the final say in who is saved. Again, make the differentiation. This is not choosing beforehand, but it is completing the act. God offers us salvation as a free gift. We decide if we want to accept it or reject it. When we decide we want it, he gives it to us. That's the final act. The Holy Spirit comes. He indwells us, He empowers us, and He helps us live for God.

It's like if we applied for a loan at the bank. The bank offers us that opportunity, we decide if we want to take advantage of it, but it's not completed until the check is in our hands.

Or, if someone has a very precious treasure, an artifact

that is worth millions of dollars, do they entrust that to just anybody? No. Only those who are proven to be trustworthy are given the opportunity. God knows if you are truly meaning it when you say you want to be saved, and He knows if you're trying to fake it. You know if you truly have the Holy Spirit living in you. You also know if he doesn't because you can't feel His power, His presence. You don't feel the joy you should have. You don't feel close to God.

1 Samuel 16:7 says man looks on the outward appearance but God looks on the heart. He knows how you really feel. He knows if you really mean business to live for Him or not.

Finally, in the last few verses (22-29) we find that God keeps His word. God keeps His word, but what has He said He will do? All those who came to Me in faith will be saved, whether Jew or Gentile. The promise, as you remember, that was given to Abraham was that "all nations will be blessed through you." He didn't say your descendants, did He? He didn't say only your offspring. He said all nations which would include the non-Israelite people.

In verses 22-26, Paul makes the point that he included the Gentiles.

> What if God—or so what if God—choosing to show His wrath and make His power known bore with great patience the object of His wrath prepared for destruction. So what if He did this to make the riches of His glory known to the object of His mercy in where He prepared in advance for glory, even us whom He called, not only from the Jews, but also from the Gentiles.

So, historically speaking, Paul says what if God offered this to one group and what if He used those who resisted and rejected to make Him more powerfully known. What if that happened? It happened for your benefit, so you can realize the strength and power of God. He did this for us, for those who are called, not only from the Jews, but the Gentiles. Anybody who witnesses the power of God and the love of God, can be saved if they choose to be.

Then Paul quotes a couple of passages from Hosea, who says that even Gentiles would be included in the family of God. He goes on further to talk about Isaiah, which reminds us that even among the Israelites would be some Christians. Not all the Israelites would be lost. Paul is mourning over the fact that Israel as a whole has rejected God. But he also recognizes the fact that among the nation of Israel, some also will be saved. He knew that the first church in Jerusalem was primarily Jewish. He knew that most of the other Apostles ministered among Jews and started churches among Jews, with a few Gentile proselytes as well.

In his own ministry, as he began it, when he went from town to town, the first place he went was to the synagogue to minister to the Jews. When he found resistance he would move out and minister to the Gentiles.

So Paul is reminding us in these verses that even though his heart is broken for his people, even among them there are those who believe and are saved.

The example of Paul reminds us of what many missionaries face when they bring the gospel to people groups in different places. Some are more receptive than others. If they find a strong resistance or defiance, they back off and go somewhere else because these people are not ready.

Paul found that to be true in his life and ministry. In some of the places he would go, he would find resistance or challenges so he would back off and go somewhere else, because God would redirect him.

As Christians, most of us know someone, or we know ourselves, in our families or among our friends, someone who has resisted the gospel and someone who is not saved and has not received any of the blessings that Paul is talking about in chapter 8. We hear stories of people praying for their loved ones for years before they're saved, if at all. Paul reminds us we should not give up. Because some people reject it now, does not mean we should stop proclaiming the gospel, the love of God. We should not diminish our responsibility to pray for them and to continue to reach out to them in love. We should continue to remind ourselves it is not up to us to get them saved. That's between them and God. All we can do is continually confront them with His love.

Everyone who hears a clear presentation of the Scriptures or the gospel plan is faced with a chance either way to accept it or to reject it. He has the freedom to choose just as the nation of Israel had the freedom to choose whether to follow God or reject God.

Our continued responsibility is to not give up. Let God do the work.

If you have never put your faith in Jesus Christ, do it today, while you still have time. Tomorrow may be too late.

If you are already a believer, do not give up on the people you know. Pray faithfully and regularly. Continue to share the gospel, taking advantage of every opportunity

CHAPTER 20

Stumbling Stone or Building Block

Today's Bible Reading: Romans 9:30 - 10:21

> As it is written: "See, I lay in Zion a stone
> that causes men to stumble and a rock
> that makes them fall, and the one who
> trusts in him will never be put to shame.
> —Romans 9:33

On our property there always seems to be tree limbs lying all over the ground. I thought it would look much nicer in our backyard to clean them all up and cut all the small bushes. So I set to work and did just that. Except, every winter more limbs and branches litter the place. After a big wind about a month ago, whole trees were added to the mess. *What should I do?* I wondered. I can't seem to keep up. Then a thought occurred to me. Since the land is very steep out back where most of the litter is, and I haven't yet got new plantings established there for the landscaping project I have in mind, why not leave most of the brush? It will slow down erosion.

The big trees I can cut up into useful lengths for future construction projects that I might have as time goes on. Those ugly trees and brush are now for me a good resource and a help in developing the lot in the future.

That is kind of what Paul is talking about here in these verses we are looking at today. Using something that appears to be evil or bad and making something good out of it. That's what God does sometimes. Is it a stumbling stone or a building block?

He starts out by saying Gentiles have received righteousness but Jews have rejected it. This is a generality. Not everyone, we realize, has rejected the gospel among the Jews, because we know that Paul himself was a Jewish Christian along with many others. The early church was established by Jewish people. But the stumbling stone over which they tripped was the simplicity of the gospel through Jesus Christ. They could not accept Him as their leader, their Lord, or as their Savior because they were too caught up in rules and regulations. So the Jews rejected Christ, as we know from history, but not all of them. A few were saved. The Gentiles have embraced Him simply because they knew no better system to approach God.

The Jewish problem was legalism, and Paul explains that in the first thirteen verses of chapter 10. Since they sought righteousness by controlling behavior, they had all sorts of rules and regulations in their books. They rejected everything from what not to do on the Sabbath to how to conduct their behavior in daily living and business transactions. They tried to control every detail of life, thinking that the more obedient they were to the law, the more righteous they would become. It didn't work. Christ said the law actually got in the way of their faith and their relationship with God.

That's true of many churches and social agencies in our world today. They try to do the same thing. They try to regulate behavior thinking it will make a better world, thinking it makes us more righteous, more in tune with God, or closer to God.

For example, some churches teach that baptism is equal to salvation. You cannot be saved unless you are baptized. They quote one or two Scripture verses and think that is a necessary thing. That work or ritual will put you in a right relationship with God. Not so. Not according to a true reading of Scripture.

Another behavior that churches teach is that people are accepted by God through participation in the sacraments. They make a big deal out of a child's first communion. They make a big deal out of not missing communion and serving communion at every meeting to be sure people have opportunity to participate and not miss out on being a part of God's kingdom.

That's just a couple of examples, but in the public realm there are also lots of social agencies that try to regulate behavior, thinking it will make us better and closer to God.

There are those people who regulate, or attempt to regulate, different aspects of life. We could name things like pornography, abortion, gambling and many other things like that which people think if they were controlled it would make us closer to God. As one person I know likes to say, "You cannot legislate morality." The change only comes about by a connection of the Holy Spirit.

Anyway, that was the stumbling block. They had so

many rules. Churches today try to make so many rules that it gets in the way of faith. This reminds me of a parody that was on the old Carol Burnett Show. You remember that one? In this particular sketch there were two men who were assigned to build a brick wall. They arrived at the sport, got out their plans and looked them over. Then they started arguing over whether or not it was correct to build the wall to the specifications. Did it meet the rules of the law? They got to bickering over the rules imposed on them by the company, the union and the community. While they are arguing, two women come along. Not knowing any better, they set to work and build the wall. When they are finished, the men were still debating the laws.

I think this clearly illustrates the concept between simple faith and rules. Let's simply approach Christ by faith, because He said true righteousness comes by actually exercising faith. Look at verses 9 and 10 of chapter 10.

No works involved. See, no works at all. Going on He says, "The Scripture says everyone who calls on the name of the Lord will be saved." This is the simple concept over which many people stumble. They can't seem to grasp that something so simple could be so wonderful.

The result for the Jewish people was that they reject God's message of salvation by faith.

Paul goes on to list a series of rhetorical questions. How can they call on someone they have never heard of? How can they hear unless someone is sent to them? And he continues on down through. Then he answers in a kind of sarcastic manner, because we see in verse 18 he asks, "Did thy not hear? Of course they did." Israel heard, Israel understood. He goes on to explain that both of those were, in fact, true.

The historical facts that he lists here are that faith comes by hearing and receiving the word of Christ (verse 17). That is a simple fact. Faith comes when you hear the gospel; you understand it and receive it for yourself. But, not all Israel accepted that good news. They heard it. They understood it. (At least most of them understood or should have understood.) Paul says that if you read the Old Testament and you read it carefully, it is understandable. They should have understood, but they didn't. They rejected it because it was just too simple.

This is true of people in our world as well. Not all citizens of our world accept the good news. The message is proclaimed all over our world and through every sort of media. We have radio, television, the printed word (Bibles, literature of all sorts). Now we have the internet which is used to proclaim the love of God to everyone, everywhere. So everyone hears the good news, and most of them can clearly understand it as it is explained in their language using simple words and phrases. Yet many, many, reject it. Thus it becomes a stumbling stone for them.

However, the stumbling stone over which many people fall can become a building block. It can become something useful, like the limbs in our backyard. Instead of tripping over them every day, we can find a useful purpose for them. People can use this simple faith to make something wonderful. If they accept this salvation by faith, that stone—that simplicity—can be a building block for a wonderful life, a wonderful relationship.

Look at chapter 9, verse 33 and what Paul says there, "The rock that makes one fall, the one who trusts in him will never be put to shame." Over in Chapter 10, verse 17, he says, "Faith comes from hearing the message through the word of Christ." Faith comes from hearing the message. Then in Acts, Peter says there is "salvation in no one else under heaven, only through Christ."

So when we accept Christ by faith it is the first step to using that block to build a better life. We know this because in 1 Corinthians 6:19, Paul himself, writing to the church at Corinth, tells us that our bodies are called the temple of the Holy Spirit. We have a house that is built by faith, a house that is established on faith. A dwelling for the Holy Spirit to live there and guide us, direct us, and teach us.

Then he says in 2 Corinthians, the first chapter, every experience we go through; whether it be difficult or good, especially the difficult times, the trials and tribulations of sickness and other bad things in life; is intended to better equip ourselves to serve others. So that building stone that we have established gives us a firm foundation on which we can build our lives for the better. Not only for ourselves, but for others, because when we have faith in Christ we look at the world differently. We don't become depressed and despondent every time something bad happens. We know there is something great in our future. We know there is something better lying ahead for us. So it gives hope. It gives us joy. It gives us peace. It gives the ability to encourage others.

That very system that was being used to make people more righteous got in the way of real faith. Rules and regulations won't work. Therefore, the people did not accept and actually rejected the simplicity of salvation by faith. That is still a stumbling block today.

Have you stumbled over the simplicity of salvation by

faith alone? It's true. It's that simple. Accept the fact that you're a sinner in need of a Savior. Believe that Jesus is that Savior you need. Confess your sinful condition, and then go on to make that former stumbling stone the foundation of your life from now on.

CHAPTER 21

Down, but Not Out

Today's Bible Reading: Romans 11:1-36

I do not want you to be ignorant, brothers,
of this mystery, so that you may not be
conceited: Israel has experienced a hardening
in part until the full number of Gentiles
has come in. And so all Israel will be
saved, as it is written: "The deliverer will
come from Zion; he will turn godlessness
away from Jacob. And this is my covenant
with them when I take away their sins.
—Romans 11:25-27

How many times have you heard someone complain, "How
can God love me after all that I have done? I'm so far down
no one could love me."

Let me read a list of people who have actually said
that: rock singer Barry McQuire, pro-wrestler Ted Dibiati,
presidential aide Chuck Colson, singer and entertainer
Glenn Campbell, and evangelist Jim Bakker. The list

could go on including housewives, businessmen, people on death row, people on drugs, alcoholics, etc. The list is almost infinite. Every day people get to the point where they say, "Who could ever love me because of all that I have done?"

Now let me read you a list of people who discovered that God is ready and willing to receive such people by his grace: rock singer Barry McQuire, pro-wrestler Ted Dibiati, presidential aide Chuck Colson, singer and entertainer Glenn Campbell, evangelist Jim Bakker and many, many others. All these discovered that God reaches them no matter how far down they have gone or how far away from Him they have turned.

Paul in this passage in Romans is dealing with that question. He is dealing with it in relation to Israel and how the Jewish people had turned their backs on God. The question arises, Will they be restored to a right relationship with Him?

Let me read what the prophet Micah said back many hundreds of years before the time of Paul. Micah writes at the end of his prophecy,

> "Who is a God like you, who pardons sins and forgives the transgressions of the remnant of his inheritance? You do not stay angry forever, but delight to show mercy. You will again have compassion on us. You will tread our sins under foot and hurl our iniquities into the depth of the sea. You will be true to Jacob and show mercy to Abraham as you pledged on oath to our fathers in days long ago."

Even Micah, so many years ago, recognized that God had in his plan a time when Israel, even though she had turned her back on God, would eventually be restored. So, the first point that Paul tries to make in this eleventh chapter is that God does not reject anyone, even though they openly and intentionally reject him for a time.

The Israelites turned their backs on Him, openly rejected Him, openly worshipped other gods, and refused to continue a close relationship with the God of their fathers; but He still loved them. As long as a person is alive, God will continue to hold out His hand of love and appeal to them for reconciliation. They may ignore God. They may reject God. They may turn away from God, but God is still right there ready to receive them back again. In 2 Peter 3:9, Peter says, "God is not willing that any should perish, but all would come to repentance." And back in the tenth chapter, the 13th verse here in Romans, what did Paul say, quoting someone earlier? He says, "Everyone who calls on the name of the Lord will be saved." That includes those who have strayed so far away, those who are down to the bottom of the pits of life.

In a family relationship, we could illustrate it this way: If there is a blended family and the father to the stepchildren is very loving, very caring, very open to receiving them, it is up to the children to receive that love. They may reject him as a replacement for their natural father, and they may not want him to be a part of their family. But if he continues to show them love, they will eventually recognize that true love is there.

So Paul says that God does not reject anyone even if they reject him. There's still an opportunity to be saved as long as you're alive and willing to recognize the plan of salvation and embrace it.

Then he goes on to say in more detail, that no one can go so far out of God's favor that they cannot be restored (verses 11-24). He talked about the olive branch and the tree there, about the Gentiles being grafted into the olive tree, representing the family of faith. He says Israel has been rejected. A lot of the natural branches were lopped off for disobedience so God brought in the Gentiles, grafted those in to make his church. They flourished and grew but there was a remnant of Israel still involved. Paul says, "I'm a Jew myself and I know other Jews who have been saved." So it wasn't an entire replacement.

So Israel, who had turned her back on God, could still come back. And Paul throughout this discourse keeps saying that over and over. That truth is the most wonderful thing! What could be better than that? If it was a good thing that the Jews were displaced so the Gentiles could hear the gospel, how much better it will be when Israel herself accepts the gospel as well. That's going to be a wonderful thing.

Going back to the idea that no one can go so far away from God that God can't reach them, let's look at a few places in the Old Testament.

In Psalm 139, David, in verses 7-12, describes trying to get away from God. If you're familiar with that passage he writes, "I tried to go into the deepest cave, God was there. High in the sky, God is there. At the bottom of the ocean, God is there. I can't get away from God no matter where I go."

Thinking about somebody who has fallen so far into sin God might not restore them, David himself and Paul the

Apostle who wrote today's text, both caused the death of innocent people, yet God received them back, blessed them, and used them mightily in service to Him.

Moses and Jonah both deliberately disobeyed a direct command from God. Yet God forgave them, received them back, and used them in his ministry to reach others with the good news that God has to offer.

In our time, you might be familiar with a story of Franklin Graham, the son of Billy Graham. He grew up in the Christian home of a world renowned evangelist, yet he rejected God and walked away for many years. Finally the Holy Spirit got a hold on him, and he was brought back. Now he is the head of a large ministry himself, a relief ministry that works all over the world. Not only helping with the pain and suffering, but bringing the good news of Jesus with it.

These are examples of people who have fallen out of favor with God, but God has restored them. God's plan includes making good of a bad situation. People reject God and Paul says that rejection sometimes turns out to be a good thing for somebody else. In the example he is using here in the discussion he is making, Israel rejected God. So God opened it up to the Gentiles. He said, "Okay, if Israel is not going to listen to Me, I'm not going to give up on the world. They were supposed to be my messengers to the world, but they failed Me. I'm not going to give up loving people. I will open the opportunity to the Gentiles. I will let them come in by faith, even as I allowed the Israelites to accept Me by faith.

Missiologists will tell you that quite often an effort is made to reach a particular people group in some part of the world only to have the people resist the gospel. They resist or reject all missionaries and foreigners. When that happens, what does the agency do? Do they try to sneak people in to soften them up? No. They back off and go somewhere else until those people are ready. Sometimes they get to the same people group by working with their neighbors. If they want to work with a tribe in central Africa, they may have to work with one or more tribes in the area, and then as they see the positive changes, the people of the original group invite them in.

When one people group resists, Christians shift resources from one area to another. The people of Summer Institute of Linguistics have been forced to back off and not work directly with the people of Colombia. The native churches they helped establish are now going to have to take more responsibilities for themselves and work more independently which may, in the long run, be a good thing. Rather than depend on outside mission support they will learn to put their trust in God. This will strengthen those churches. It will encourage them to be stronger in God as a church and as individuals within the church.

So Paul asks, What has God done? Has he given up on Israel? By no means! Have they gone so far out of God's favor that they cannot be brought back? No way.

That's true of everybody that you and I might know. God has not given up on them, and they have not gone so far away that they cannot be brought back. God still loves them. God still wants them. God is still ready to receive them when they are ready to come home.

In a quote from this discussion about the olive tree, F.F. Bruce writes this:

The olive tree in this analogy is the true Israel, the people of God; the branches are its individual members. Because of unbelief some of the branches were cut out, and their place taken by branches from a wild olive or orleaster - Gentile believers - who were grafted on to the stock of Israel to shape its vitality and nourishment. But these newly engrafted branches had no cause for pride: by faith they had been grafted in, but by unbelief they would be cut out like many of the original branches. By now the analogy with horticultural practice has been strained to the limit, but the link snaps completely when Paul says that God can graft the original branches, which were lopped off back on to their parent tree, to derive life from it anew. Paul seriously expects such a miracle of grace in the spiritual realm and illustrates it by what would be a miracle in the natural realm.

Paul closes the discussion about all he has said concerning Israel, beginning in verse 25, by saying that Israel will one day be restored to her former glory, her close relationship with God as a nation, as a people. In verse 25 he says, "I don't want you to be ignorant about this mystery, so you won't be conceited." This is the second time he has warned the Gentiles not to think they are better than the Jewish people because we all stand by faith, we enter the church by faith even though Israel has stumbled over the stumbling stone, as we talked about earlier. Don't get arrogant. Don't get prideful. That would be a sin, and you would be in danger of judgment from God for that. He says, "I want you to be aware of this." Israel is experiencing a hardening, not all Israel, but a large part, until the full number of Gentiles has come in. In other words, Paul's theology said that God had set a quota for the last Gentile to believe. We don't know the size of that number or if it's actually a number or some other method of calculation. Apparently, Paul believed that at some point God's going to say, "Okay, we're full. Let's bring it to a close. Let's bring everybody home."

Then Paul says, "A deliverer will come from Zion. He will turn godlessness away from Jacob, and this is my covenant with them when I take away their sins." This is a quote from Isaiah 59, talking about when Christ himself sits on a throne in Israel and the Jewish people actually accept him as their Lord and Messiah.

That is the point when Israel as a people will believe. That is when Israel will be restored. The branches that had been broken off are brought back onto the tree. That is going to be a wonderful time in human history. A time when God himself will reign on earth and all the world lives in peace. Jews and Gentiles will be living together for they will all be blessed.

When other people groups see Christians making a positive impact on their society, they are going to want to embrace Christianity. Unfortunately, history tells us that people who claim the name of Christ often don't follow through. They don't make a good impression on the world because they don't really live like they claim to believe.

But you and I need to be faithful to God. We need to make a positive impact. We need to present Christ's love, his grace, his mercy, and his power so people will want it for themselves.

This whole concept of what God is willing to do, the

whole book of Romans up to this point is where Paul discusses many of the doctrines of the church, and over and over again he has expressed salvation by faith as the basic element.

From chapter 1 really, up to now, he says salvation is by faith and that's the most important thing.

We don't fully understand all of God's workings, his understanding, his wisdom. We can't comprehend all that. It's too wonderful, too big, too amazing for us. Who would think that God himself, would reach out and heal a woman who was full of demons and a prostitute, receive her, and redeem her to himself? Who would think that he would take somebody who is homeless and an alcoholic, living on the streets with no future in sight? Yet he can turn that person around and change him/her into an evangelist, a Sunday school teacher, or someone who touches many lives for Christ.

That's beyond our comprehension. Many of us wouldn't even speak to these kinds of people. Many of us wouldn't even want to associate with these kinds of people. God does. He wants to restore these people. He wants to bring them to himself. We need to remind ourselves that that person, even in our families or among the people we know who have walked away from God and are going through terrible times, have not gone too far to find grace. They can be brought into the family of God. If they've ever known God, that relationship can be restored, made wonderful and whole again.

"Who," he says, "has known the knowledge and wisdom of God?" How unsearchable are His judgments and His ways beyond finding out! Who has been God's counselor?

Certainly not I. He's a lot wiser than I am. For from Him and through Him and to Him are all things including salvation by grace. To Him be given the glory and the power for ever and ever.

CHAPTER 22

Sacrificial Lamb or Token Gift

Today's Bible Reading: Romans 12:1, 2

"Therefore, I urge you, brothers, in view
of God's mercy, to offer your bodies as
living sacrifices, holy and pleasing to
God - this is your spiritual act of worship.
Do not conform any longer to the pattern
of this world, but be transformed by the
renewing of your mind. Then you will be
able to test and approve what God's will
is - his good, pleasing and perfect will.
—Romans 12:1, 2

In Mark's Gospel we read, "Jesus sat down opposite the place where the offerings were put and watched the crowd putting their money into the temple treasury. Many rich people threw in large amounts. But a poor widow came and put in two very small copper coins, worth only a fraction of a penny."

Calling his disciples to him, Jesus said, "I tell you the

truth, this poor widow has put more into the treasury then all the others. They all gave out of their wealth; but she, out of her poverty, put in everything—all she had to live on."

Some gave a fraction; the widow gave all. Mark places this incident at the end of a series of illustrations through which Jesus emphasized the need of an *attitude* that is pleasing to God more than *actions* that make us look good.

In the story of the widow, his point is that we should be willing to give our last dime, everything we have to God for his service.

Paul says we should do this "in view of God's mercy." John 3:16 says that God loved the world so much he was willing to sacrifice his Son. Back in Romans 5:6 and 8 we are told that Christ died for the ungodly, the just for the unjust. Going way back to Isaiah (vv. 53:4-6, 10a) we read that Christ was the sacrifice offered on our behalf.

My Random House dictionary defines mercy as compassionate or kindly forbearance shown toward an offender, an enemy, or other person in one's power. In other words it is something good done on our behalf that we don't deserve. What God did for us was the ultimate act of mercy.

The first eleven chapters of Romans describe what God has done for us. He proved himself to us, sacrificed himself for us, and provides himself as a way out of degradation and misery. In light of all he has done for us, we should give ourselves wholly to him as sacrificial lambs, not just token offerings that cost us nothing.

Drawing from Old Testament practices in Jewish history, we know two things about sacrificial lambs. First, we know that any animal offered for sacrifice must be given without reservation. That is, the giver cannot, once he has presented his gift, decide to take it back. Can you imagine the uproar it would have caused in the temple if a man presented his lamb for slaughter, and then suddenly grabbed it back from the priest, claiming it was his last one and he couldn't spare it? What sacrilege! To bring a lamb for sacrifice was an act of worship honoring Almighty God, and no one dared to take it back.

Yet many people in our churches today do that very thing. They present themselves and all they have to the Lord, and then when they realize it will actually cost them something, they want to take it back. They would rather be like the contented rich people in Mark's illustration, giving some token amount instead of all. Is it any less sacrilegious for us to keep back what we promised to God?

Paul's response was that giving fully of ourselves without reservation (and without changing our minds) is only reasonable in light of all that God has done for us. When we recognize his greatness, his goodness, and his mercy all directed toward us; we should be humbled, grateful, and so respectful of Him we would worship him by offering the only thing we truly have of our own—our lives.

A second thing we know about sacrificial lambs is that they must be clean, pure, and healthy. By presenting them to the Lord, they also become holy.

We can be made clean, pure, and healthy, both in mind and body, by listening to and obeying the principles, precepts, and commands of Scripture. Many of these are clearly spelled out and easy to understand and apply. When the Bible says, "Do not steal," we know what that means and how to accomplish it. Other things are life principles that take time and discipline to develop. Many of them also require us to lean heavily on the Spirit to fulfill our task. Can any of us truly say we love all our neighbors, let alone our enemies? I think we all know someone who seems to be hard to get along with or "unlovable."

That's why it's important to be in the Scriptures every day. Reading, studying, and meditating on a few verses at a time will help us to gradually understand what God expects from us. Our minds will slowly become acquainted with the ways of God, and our actions will reflect the love and compassion of God more and more.

This process is not unlike the educational and social development of children. If we expect them to be responsible, caring citizens when they become adults, then we must see that they learn what society expects of them, beginning with basics and teaching them how to deal with more complex issues as they grow and their minds expand. We do not expect a second grader to think and act like a high school student. Nor do we expect high school students to behave like mature adults. It takes time, training, and experience to develop maturity.

Spiritually speaking it takes time, training and experience to mature as well. The process of becoming clean, pure, and healthy in God's sight is not instantaneous for most of us. We struggle with habits, thoughts, and personal issues that just don't seem to go away. But as we grow and mature we learn how to "put them away" like childish toys we no longer play with.

One aspect of the Christian life that I think is not emphasized enough is the area of holiness. As I understand the concept in Scripture, to be holy is to be set apart for the Lord's use and service. Yet most of us cling to our old ways, our old manners, our old systems which are, in a true analysis, selfishly motivated. I want a bigger, more active church. I want attention. I want people to notice me or my ministry. This kind of thinking really is not submissive to the Lord's will or leading. It is putting me in the driver's seat, hoping to get to the winner's circle.

To be truly set apart from the world and "old man" thinking, we need to learn to let go of all the sinful, selfish thoughts and allow the Spirit to transform us into people who think more in terms of service. A truly servant attitude will develop as we learn to care less about who gets the credit and more about meeting the needs of the people, both physically and spiritually.

If we want our lives to be truly acceptable sacrifices for the Lord, we must not only give our entire selves, but we must do our best, with the help of the Holy Spirit, to keep ourselves clean, pure, healthy, and holy since God will accept nothing less.

As believers in the Lord Jesus Christ, Paul is asking us to offer ourselves to the Lord for service completely, unreservedly and perfectly, just as a lamb used to be brought to the temple.

How committed are you? Have you given yourself sacrificially or as a token gift? Are you living for God, who did so much for you or for yourself?

Will you do as Paul requests? Will you offer your life to the Lord to be used however and wherever He directs? In light of all He has done for you, this is only a reasonable response. If your answer is yes, then mean it. Show you mean it by committing yourself to apply the Scriptures to your everyday life. Get involved in ministry for ministry sake not for any reward or glory.

As the old hymn says, "Give of your best to the Master." Why not give Him your life today? Commit your life to His service, and He will bless you mightily and make you a blessing to many.

CHAPTER 23

Two Signs of a Renewed Mind

Today's Bible Reading: Romans 12:3-21

"For by the grace given to me I say to every one of you: Do not think of yourself more highly than you ought, but rather think of yourself with sober judgment, in accordance with the measure of faith God has given you.
—Romans 12:3

Dana Perkins, who makes regular teacher training trips to Russia, told us in a recent letter some members of the Russian government accuse Christians of mind-controlling tactics to gain followers. While their accusation is false on the part of the pastors and teachers, within the true Christian church the concept is not far off. Paul tells us here that we should have our minds renewed. We should start over. We should have a new way of living, a new way of looking at life, and not be conformed to the patterns of this world.

It is a real part of biblical theology that says that anyone who accepts Christ by faith must undergo a mind-changing experience. You have to. There's no escaping it.

Jesus said, "You must be born again." By that he meant you must wipe the old slate clean and start over with a new attitude and a new approach to live.

Paul wrote in Ephesians the fourth and fifth chapters, "Put off the old man with its sinful nature and put on a new man that is controlled by the Holy Spirit." Here in the book of Romans (chapters 6 & 8), we have already seen that Paul teaches that a believer must be totally and completely immersed in service to Christ, if he is, in fact, their Lord and Savior.

Now Paul begins to teach us in more detail what it actually means to be renewed in our minds and having our actions reflect that renewal. He says that we will be discussing two basic tests or signs that our minds have been renewed by the Holy Spirit.

The first is humility. A real sign of a Christian's devotion to God is humility. That is, not as a lot of people think, being a rug for everybody else to walk over. Humility does not mean giving up your rights, your position and your place in favor of everybody else and being the last in line every time. It doesn't mean that. It doesn't mean accepting a put down every time someone wants to demean you.

A truly humble person recognizes his place within the larger framework of life as well as the position of others and working with that in mind. True humility says I recognize my place and I know your place. I want to bless both; I want to encourage both. I want to show you I believe you and I are both worth something in the sight of God.

Humility recognizes that no one of us can do everything. There are pastors and church ministry leaders who do not recognize that fact. They think they must run everything down to the last detail. That has never been my practice. I recognize and I know it's biblical to recognize that the work of the ministry has to be divided among qualified people. When a pastor recognizes someone as qualified for a position or the leadership of his church recognizes that and they ask someone to fill a position, they should allow them the freedom to conduct that area of ministry without asking every five minutes, "What are you doing? How can you change? Why didn't you tell me this?" and all that kind of thing. No one can do everything so we must recognize that others need to share the burden. Everyone has a special place in God's church.

Paul here, as he does in 1 Corinthians, uses the analogy of the physical body. Look at your body. Would it be whole or function properly if some of the major parts were missing? No. Can my eyes do the function of a hand? No. Could I stand up very well if I didn't have any feet? No. These things are important. They are part of the whole and each part is important. We each have different gifts according to the grace that God has given us, and we need to recognize that in ourselves and in each other. That's what humility does. It recognizes the place of each one within the church.

It also teaches us to let others serve without unnecessary hindrance (verses 6-8). We have different gifts, and if a man's gift is prophesying *let him do that*. If it is serving, *let him serve*. If it's teaching, *let him teach*. The same goes for encouraging, giving, being hospitable and all these things Paul puts in this list. We must not criticize people negatively who are doing something we cannot do. If I'm not qualified to be a teacher of children, who am I to say a child's teacher is doing it wrong unless there is something obvious going on? Who am I to say a person is not a good singer, if I am tone deaf? If a person is gifted as a musician or singer, let him/her sing or play the music to the glory of God and within the church of God and not be unduly critical of it.

This does not mean we shall not offer corrections or suggestions when appropriate and necessary. These are important as well to help keep each one on track, but we should not criticize someone negatively who is doing something we are not qualified to do. That would bring down the church rather than build it up. True humility, Paul says, builds up each other. You think of the other person as a gifted person and you encourage him/her and help out as much as you can.

Don't think of yourself more highly than you ought to think, but rather think of yourself with sober judgment. In other words, take an honest assessment of yourself. Know what you're qualified to do, and then do it. At the same time, recognize the gifts of other people. Know what they are qualified to do and encourage them to do it well. Let him teach. Let him encourage. Let him give. Let him share. Let him do his work within the ministry without undue criticism. That's a lesson that many Christian people have never learned, unfortunately. We offer negative criticism constantly, and it should not be happening.

When our minds are transformed to where we get true humility, we're going to encourage God's people to do their ministries and do them well, not tear them down.

What God is asking of us (through Paul) is not normal.

It is not a part of normal human thinking. It is easy for us to criticize. It is so easy for us to point out the negatives or the bad side of somebody, to gossip, or pass around stories and rumors. When our minds are renewed, every time a bad thought comes into our heads regarding another fellow Christian, we should say a prayer of forgiveness and ask God to rid us of these thoughts. We should not let them come out of our mouths, not let them spread bad things, and if they do, we should be quick to beg forgiveness and seek reconciliation.

A second sign that Paul discusses is love (vv. 9-21). In this list he gives nineteen examples of love. He shows how love can be shown as a sign of our renewed minds. Some of the things he discusses on this list, again are not normal things for people to do.

Love, as Paul shows us in the 13th chapter of 1 Corinthians, is very unselfish. He says that again here. Chapter 12 of Romans is almost a repeat of chapter 13 in 1 Corinthians. Paul is writing to a different church so he rewords it just as we would if we wrote two letters to different people on the same subject. We would not use the identical writing. Neither does Paul.

The subject is the same here. He starts out by saying it must be sincere. There are three groups of people that he discusses in these verses. The first is others in ministry. We must learn to love others in ministry and be devoted to one another. Honor one another above ourselves. So true love toward a fellow minister, a fellow servant of God means there are four things we should do. We should pray for them, we should encourage them, we should assist them in any way we can, and we should give them honest and loving feedback regarding their ministries to help them improve and help them walk closer to God.

When we show genuine love, we're going to build up one another, we're going to encourage one another, and we're going to pray for one another for that is showing how we care and how much we appreciate their ministries.

Something I try to do every year at least once to encourage people in my ministry is to give them a note of encouragement. I do appreciate everyone I have worked with and all that they have done, and I thank God for bringing them to me to be part of my ministry. I pray that we will be able to serve Him together for a long time to come.

We shall be not only doing that for each other on a regular basis—praying, encouraging, assisting and caring—but also for these people to whom we minister, the ones that sit under our ministries, whatever it might be. For the teacher, it is the ones in the classroom. For those who contribute to the needs of others, it would be those needy people. For the ones in leadership, it is all of the membership and those who attend worship and participate in the various ministries. Those we minister to should be shown genuine love as well.

Paul says we should do that by never being lacking in zeal or enthusiasm. Always be enthusiastic about your ministry. If you're in it because you love to do it, it's going to show. If you're doing it just because it needs to be done, that's going to show too. You're not going to be as excited about it as you ought to be because your heart's not in it.

"Never be lacking in enthusiasm, but keep your spiritual fervor," he says. "Be joyful in hope, patient in afflictions, faithful in prayer." Keep up the excitement. Learn to be patient with the people you work with. Learn to be careful. Listen closely to them. Understand them. Get to know them outside the areas of ministry so you can really meet their needs in a better way. Be involved in their lives. Never become proud or arrogant. He says, "Do not be conceited." Be willing to associate with people of low estate or those who are not always appreciated in this world.

I've seen many occasions where people come into an assembly, take a seat, and just like oil and water, everybody else scatters because they didn't want to sit by so-and-so. They didn't appreciate the way he dressed or the way she smelled or whatever, but that person is still a soul that God loves and we should learn to love them with the same unconditional love that He had and still has. We should embrace them and accept them. Never become proud or arrogant because you are not any better than he or she in the sight of God.

God saved you by grace when you were a part of the sinful world. If you do reject them, if you do shun them, if you do avoid them, you may be shutting somebody out of the kingdom of God. That's a sin you have to deal with between yourself and God.

We must show genuine love to our fellow ministers, those in service, but we also must show genuine love to those to whom we minister in the larger ministry and in our focused ministries as well.

Thirdly, Paul ends this discourse by talking about showing love towards those who work actively against us. He quotes two passages of Scripture. One is from the Old Testament where he quotes the phrase, "Vengeance is mine, says the Lord, I will repay." Don't try to get even. Don't try to fight them on their ground. Leave it to God.

Then he quotes Jesus, who says, "If your enemy is hungry, feed him. If he's thirsty, give him something to drink. In doing this you will be heaping coals on his head."

Genuine love for people who are operating actively against our ministries means we should pray for them. They need God. They need the love of God. They need to have their minds changed.

We should never seek revenge, but leave that to God in his own time. It may come soon. It may come later. It may not even come until the final judgment. That's not up to us to decide.

We can reach out to them. We should embrace them. We should show them love and acceptance on God's terms.

That means we should never aggravate points of disagreement. How it breaks my heart to see Christians openly defying the law, challenging people to a fight. That's not biblical! Christians should be trying to avoid confrontation. Yes, we should stand up for what the Bible says. Yes, we should encourage people to believe Scripture and live by Scripture, but the Bible also says, right here and in other places, be careful to do what is right in the eyes of everybody, if it is possible. "As far as it depends on you, live at peace with everyone." That means, don't beg for a fight. That means if a challenge is put out there, try to negotiate it through peaceful means.

Now that could be brought out in many different ways, but I believe people who openly beg for a fight are breaking Scripture and are actually making a bad name for Christianity.

Paul says we should pray for our enemies. We should try to live and work with them in a peaceful manner. Don't try to take revenge. Do not seek a challenge and prove the other guy wrong, because that's not love.

Love says, "I wish you understood the truth of Scripture. I wish you could understand how much God loves you. I wish you would listen to both sides and would listen to how much the truth of Scripture can change your life."

We should learn to treat our enemies with respect and dignity, because they are people that God loves as much as ourselves. They may be unbelievers in need of love and someone to love them. Their resistance to God and their opposition to the gospel might be out of a true need for love and acceptance. They may have never experienced it before. Or they may be believers who have not been genuinely loved by anyone else other than God. There are those within the larger church of God by faith, who still bring up problems and stir agitations simply because they don't know what true love is. They think by keeping things moving, keeping things active, they don't have to worry about being lonely, shut out or ignored.

True love says we care. We want you to be part of the kingdom. We want to work peacefully with you.

Paul in this chapter says two signs of a renewed mind are true humility and genuine acceptance. Humility is knowing your place in the church and recognizing the place of others; and learning to encourage others, to bless them and to share with them and love them.

If our minds are renewed by the Spirit of God, we're not to shut people out. We're not going to put people down. We are going to lift them up and embrace them, because that's what God does.

We should not be overcome by evil, but overcome the evil and the bad things with good, with love.

CHAPTER 24

Civil Obedience

Today's Bible Reading: Romans 13:1-7

"Everyone must submit himself to the
governing authorities for there is no
authority except that which God has
established. The authorities that exist
have been established by God."
—Romans 13:1, 2

Last week in my mail was an appeal for Christians to
participate in a public demonstration against a practice
currently allowed by law. It was intended to be a peaceful
demonstration on the steps of our capitol. I assume it turned
out that way since I heard nothing contrary on the news.
This week I received another appeal. This time it was to
pack a hearing room in Augusta to challenge the possible
treatment of a minority group from what has already been
established as common practice. People who want others to

gather there want equal and fair treatment for all rather than show special favors for one group.

Now these appeals and other calls to action for us as Christians force us to ask ourselves some critical questions. Should Christians be involved in politics? That is the central question we all have to ask ourselves and if we say yes, how far should we go? How deep into politics should we be involved? What activities are allowed by biblical principles and what are not?

I think Paul answers some of those questions here in Romans 13. He starts out by saying, "Everyone must submit himself to the governing authorities for there is no authority except that which is allowed by God." That is a very simple and straightforward statement that leaves little room to question how to interpret it. Everyone must submit himself to the governing authorities because God has put them there. Is that enough said?

Well, there's actually more to the question than that. So Paul tries to explain it a little bit, and if we look in other parts of Scripture, we see other relevant points. He says in his explanation that the authorities that exist have been put there by God. Consequently, if we rebel against authority, we are rebelling against what God has established. What Paul is saying is that if you actively and intentionally resist or reject governing authorities, you find yourself in defiance of God himself.

Now, we have to ask ourselves, What constitutes rebellion in Paul's mind? Is that the same thing as defiance of the law? Is that the same thing as civil disobedience? Are those forms of rebellion, or do we want to draw lines and say each one is distinctly different?

Well, it depends. What does Scripture teach us about our relationship to authority? Should we break the law through civil disobedience? The very word disobedience says there is a violation of some sort. If you're disobeying a law, you're breaking it, right? That's a minor form of rebellion. Open rebellion is when you gather people together, arm them and try to overthrow the government. Defiance might mean you don't want to submit, you don't want to obey the law. You don't make a big scene unless challenged, but quietly refuse to obey. So defiance itself may not be open rebellion, but it may be resistance.

What Paul is saying here is that anyone who defies the law or breaks the law on purpose is rebelling against God. That means that Christian people and so called Christian organizations should always operate within the law, not break the law in their procedures or activities. Everything a Christian does and every Christian organization, whether it is social, political, or religious should operate under the laws of the country in which they are established.

There is one exception and that is clearly pointed out by Scripture. When Peter and John were arrested, what exception did they disclose? I cannot obey the law if it keeps me from sharing the Gospel. I must present the Gospel even if the law says no. That law may be broken, and God would not be offended.

We heard from our friend, Dana, that in Russia they are clamping down on Christians. We have heard from people in other countries like Colombia that they are clamping down on Christians. China has a very strict rule regarding who can meet and where, trying to control activities of not only Christians, but other groups as well. Those believers, as much as possible, should operate within the law unless it says they cannot share their faith. Then they have the right, under God's authority, to break the law.

We should be operating as much as possible within the law and the legal system that we have. Here in America, we have opportunities within our political system to be involved in the process to continue to allow freedom of religion, freedom to share the Gospel, freedom to do what needs to be done. Our political process allows us to be involved at any and every level. We might simply go to the voting booth once or twice a year. Or it might be to the extent that some Christians have gone to actually run for office and to be involved on a daily basis in the legislative system, in making the laws or preventing the bad laws from being made.

We have that freedom and I personally believe that God would expect us to take advantage of those opportunities as far as we are qualified. If someone is comfortable only going to the voting booth once or twice a year, that's fine. If someone else feels convicted enough to want to be active in trying to change things, they should as long as they operate within the law. That's their right and privilege, and I think God has given us those freedoms and rights.

Paul says rulers, leaders, or the government under which we operate are there, not as a threat to those who intentionally break the law, but as a blessing to those who obey it. So if Christians under any legal system want to prevent a confrontation with their government, they should, as much as possible, operate under the law.

Simply he said, if we operate under the law, we are no threat. But if we break the law the enforcers are there to restrict illegal activity, and it is their responsibility to control that.

If we truly treat our civil authorities with Christlike biblical love, will they really have any reason to punish us? Will they really have any reason to clamp down on Christian activities if the people involved in those activities are showing real love as it is described in chapter 13 of 1 Corinthians where love, it tells us, is unconditional giving for the benefit of the other person? What government wants to restrict the activities of people who are a benefit or a blessing to their society? Some do because they are mistaken in their philosophy. They are mistaken in what Christians represent. These Christians who truly bring a blessing with them will be accepted, will be honored, and will be allowed to operate. Of course we have to keep in mind that God does establish and put in place authorities and powers on purpose to control the activities of people. We have seen from Scripture how God manipulates governments to his advantage. We should always keep that in mind as well.

So Paul says everyone must submit himself to the governing authorities because they are there by God's design and will. Therefore if we break the rules of the land, we are defying God.

Then he goes on to say that that's not the only reason. Another reason is that your conscience should tell you that you're doing wrong. Christians should submit to governing authorities because our consciences tell us we must.

Now, our conscience is that part of us, as human beings, that God has given to each one of us that recognizes right and wrong. It makes us feel guilty when we know we are doing wrong and warns us in times of temptations to avoid doing wrong. The conscience is that part of us, as some people say, that is a little bit of God inside of you. I wouldn't personally use that expression, but we know everyone has one, and it is given to us at creation by God himself. We also know from Scripture and from experience, that some people's consciences get very, very hard. They almost appear like they have none.

We can call the conscience, for lack of a better term, our moral barometers that tell us when we are headed for trouble. We should pay attention. When we follow God, our consciences should be activated every time something questionable arises. Your conscience will say, "You know that is wrong, so don't do it." Then you will have to decide which to obey, your conscience or the law. In the case of evangelism, because God has said it's okay and you know you're going to break the law when you speak to someone about Christ, your conscience is clear because it is God who made your conscience and it is to Him you have to answer someday. Your conscience then overrules the law.

Our consciences are designed by God and they are influenced by the Holy Spirit. They only operate when we are faced with something God would not approve of. He lists several examples of when people's consciences might bother them. When you pay taxes, does your conscience bother you if you don't send in the right amount? It should. If you fudge the tax form to make your income look lower? It should. If you owe taxes, pay your taxes. Pay the full amount without question or hesitation. It is your responsibility not only to the government, but to God. It helps support the government that God has put into place.

Give everyone what you owe. Not only your taxes, but

if you borrow money from a lending agency or from anyone else, be sure to pay it back. Pay it on time whenever possible and with any interest due. If you borrowed it in good faith, you should expect to pay it back.

If you owe someone respect, then give them the respect they deserve. That's people in any leadership position or even in your own household. We're told that wives should honor and respect their husbands, husbands should honor and respect their wives, and all of us should respect people who are in positions of authority. Give them respect.

How many times have I cringed when I have heard people criticize the presidents of our country in ways that are very demeaning? We may not like the decisions they make, or even them as individuals, but as our president, they deserve our respect.

Governors should be treated the same way. The same thing is true of other leaders in government. I've heard people say, why is so-and-so on the town board or committee? He can't even run his own business. That's disrespect. He may not deserve to be in office, but if you didn't vote against him you allowed him to be there. So give the respect he or she deserves.

If honor, then honor. The list goes on.

We should give our leaders everything they deserve politically and socially, within the church and within our own homes. They are there by God's allowance, God's permission, God's choice. So we should give them everything we owe them.

So when we are faced with a challenge to decide between our government and God, who should we follow? God. When we are faced with the decision of which is right, this law or my own impressions, my own feelings, which is right? The law.

Paul says we should honor these people. We should submit to these people. It goes back to the point he makes in the larger scope of this discussion that we should, as often as possible, live at peace with everybody. "As much as it is in you," he said, "learn to live in peace with everybody."

We need to do that as a church as well as individual Christians. Throughout history Christianity has done some really stupid things, to put it bluntly, things people thought they were doing in the name of God and with God's blessing, which, in fact, turned the world against Christianity. We could look at the Crusades when they slaughtered millions of people because they refused to become Christians on the spot. Or we could look at our own country, in our own time, where people openly participate in riots on the street just to prove a point. That puts a black mark on the Christian name. There are many other things we have done. We need to learn the lesson Paul is telling those people in Rome. They didn't have it much easier than we do. They were living under a government that did not like Jews. They were living under a government that did not accept Christianity. They were living under a government that thought that every group that met without a government representative might be a group that tried to promote rebellion. Yet Paul says to submit, obey, and live at peace. That's what we should do.

Yes, I believe Christians should be involved in politics. Every Christian should be involved to the level where he or she is comfortable because God has given us that privilege.

Every one of us should live under the law unless the law defies the right to share your faith.

How do you view those in authority? Are you afraid of the police? Do you exercise your rights to be involved in the political system of your state and country? In all you do show respect for those in authority. At the same time continue to do what you feel God has called you to do to improve your society, including sharing the Good News of Jesus.

CHAPTER 25

One Debt You Cannot Pay

Today's Bible Reading: Romans 13:8-10

"Love does no harm to its neighbor.
Therefore, love is the fulfillment of the law."
—Romans 13:10

There is no one who is debt-free in this world. No one at all. No matter how well off you may be or think you are, no matter how much wealth you may have accumulated, how big your bank account is, how many accounts you have, you are not debt-free, especially if you are a Christian. You may not owe anyone any money. You may not have any loans outstanding. You may not have borrowed anything from a friend or neighbor that needs to be returned. Yet you still owe something. You have the debt of love.

Paul has just discussed the Christian's relationship with four different groups of people in the verses leading up to this point. He says we need to have a good relationship with other believers, and we need to show respect and honor to unbelievers. We need to show respect to those who are opposing our faith. He goes on to say we need to show respect and honor to those in authority. Four groups of people that we need to show patience, respect, and honor to.

Now, he says that as a group, we Christians need to be characterized by love—unconditional love. This is not love that says, "I'll love you if you love me," or love that says, "I want something in return for what I do for you." No, our love should be unconditional love.

Why did he use the phrase "you are in debt to love one another?" Do we really owe love to anybody?

Why should I show love to those people or to that person I know doesn't even like me or are doing things that are just the opposite of what I represent and stand for? Why should I show love to those people who want to wipe out Christianity?

Scripture gives two clear reasons why. Paul says in these verses that when we show unconditional love, we are fulfilling the law. What was the law? Well, he lists several that were pulled out of the Ten Commandments.

Now, if we go back to that list of Ten Commandments in Exodus 20, we see that it is divided into two basic groups. The first four commandments are focused on God. He says we should honor, respect, and obey God. We should worship Him only and no one else. Four commandments are focused on God and come first on the list.

In this letter to the Romans, we have already seen in three different passages where Paul says we need to be fully committed to God if we are Christians, if we have been born again and received Him as our Savior. He wants all of us, not just our minds, not just an hour on Sunday morning, not just part of us. He wants our whole being.

So the law says we need to be fully committed to God. If we are fully committed to God, then the second part of the law comes into play, the last six commandments which deal with our relationships to other people. This is what Paul focuses on here, the relationships with other people. The commandments he lists and a few others talk about what we should not be doing to other people or what we would like them not to do to us.

Now in the Good Samaritan story in Luke chapter 10, what was Jesus's answer to the question, "Who is my neighbor?" It's that person who needs me, right? It's that person out there I can help. He is my neighbor, and I should be a good neighbor to him/her by providing the help I am capable of giving. Whether it is physical, as it was in that story, financial, spiritual, or any other way; it doesn't matter. We should be showing love to them. You are keeping the law of God if you show unconditional love, if you reach out to that neighbor, that friend, that fellow worker who needs love, who needs to know God. One basic reason for showing unconditional love is that the law says we should. It's fulfilling the law or keeping the law by doing that.

Now, when we say unconditional love, let's examine that for a minute. We have stated in general terms to mean anyone out there who needs love. But what about that person I just can't get along with? What about that person at work that irritates me every time I meet him/her? How can I show love toward that person? What about the new neighbor who moved in and lives a lifestyle that you know is blatantly wrong according to Scripture? He might be a homosexual, might be one who lives in open sexual immorality, or has loud drunken parties every weekend. How are you going to reach out in love to those kinds of people? How can you love the kind of person who lives a lifestyle totally different from your own? These are questions you have to ask God, you have to settle in your own mind, and you have to deal with because these people are a part of your lives. For every situation, for each individual, the approach will be a little different. You have to find the way that works for you within God's will. That does not mean we should back off and ignore them. If that gay neighbor needs help, should we refuse it just because they live that kind of lifestyle? Unconditional loves says no.

Are you going to refuse to help that person who works in an abortion agency just because that is where they work? Unconditional love will say no. You will reach out and help them anyway.

You are fulfilling the commands of God when you reach out and show unconditional love. Love does no harm to his neighbor. It is the fulfillment of the law.

Scripture also points out another reason why we should reach out to others with unconditional love. It is because when we show unconditional love, we are accepting those people as people of worth in the eyes of God.

How many people did Christ reject because He didn't like the way they lived? None. To how many people did Christ say, "You come to the cross, and I won't let you in because of who you are?" None. None at all.

God created every single individual who has ever lived, and the Bible teaches us that He created them in his image. They are fellow servants and sinners with us. He sees each one as precious in His sight, just as precious as you and I. When he went to the cross he said he was dying for the whole world, not a select group. In essence he said I want everyone to be saved. I want everyone to come to me for help, hope and assurance. There is no exception to John 3:16 that says "whosoever comes will be saved." Isaiah 53:6 is a good verse to remind us that we are all equal, where that prophet wrote, "We are all like sheep that have gone astray. We have turned everyone to his way, yet the Lord has laid on them the iniquity of us all." We are all sinners. We are no better than that guy next door or down the street. We all deserve punishment, but God offers grace.

In the New Testament, Paul talks on several occasions about developing the mind of Christ, becoming a new man in Christ. Now we can do that when we acquire a strong desire to see people saved. That is part of having the mind of Christ. He didn't want anyone to be rejected or left out and neither should we.

When we show love and compassion to our fellow man, no matter who he is, we are reaching out the same way Christ reached out, with unconditional love.

I love you because God loves you. I love you because you are someone God made and He made you precious and special. He made you like me, a sinner in need of a Savior. I love you because of that.

When we show hatred, disregard and disinterest to people just because we don't understand them or we don't like the way they live or what they do, we are judging them and concluding they are not worthy of God's love. That's wrong.

We should learn to live unconditionally. It's not an

easy lesson. It's not an easy thing to do because, naturally speaking, we want to shut out those people we don't like, those whose lifestyles we don't like, don't agree with, or don't want to be close to. It's easy to walk away.

Christ never said the Christian life would be easy. He said, "I challenge you to go and make disciples of all people everywhere." No exceptions. So as Christian people we need to go above and beyond what other people do. We need to stand out from the world by showing unconditional love. The kind of love that says, "I welcome you just as you are to learn of this Savior who loves me."

Being unselfishly different, being totally different from the world. The world says, "I will love those who love me, those who give me something in return for my love." Christ said it exemplified being friends of the lowly, the outcast, the rejected people, those who need help and hope.

When we separate ourselves into Christ, when we become like Christ, we will be different. We will stand out from the world. When we do that we will show the world what it means to show love unconditionally. Unconditional love is unselfish love.

Paul explains love very thoroughly and very carefully in 1 Corinthians 13. The challenge for us is to pass on that love. The debt of love can't be repaid, but regularly, daily, we can reach out and show love to someone who needs it.

CHAPTER 26

This Do in Anticipation of Me

Today's Bible Reading: Romans 13:11-14

"Let us behave decently, as in the daytime
not in orgies and drunkenness, not in
sexual immorality and debauchery, not
in dissention and jealousy. Rather, clothe
yourselves with the Lord Jesus Christ,
and do not think about how to gratify
the desires of the sinful nature."
—Romans 13:13, 14

I was talking to some friends recently about a situation that occurs in many places of business. Notice had been given that a delegation from the district office or headquarters was going to show up to inspect the premises. Immediately everybody started scrambling. They cleaned, polished and scrubbed. They did everything they could to make it nice and neat and tidy for them when they came. Everyone is supposed to look busy, active and productive in front of these people when they come. There should be an appearance of everything being done exactly according to company policy regarding safety, efficiency and service.

The truth is that in between visits everybody slacks off. They don't pay a lot of attention to the policies. Cleaning is not always thorough. Safety is not always top priority. Policies are often ignored or overlooked in favor of efficiency or speed. Getting the quantity out and just getting by in other areas is status quo.

That's the kind of situation that Paul says we should avoid. That attitude of hurry up and clean up. Instead, he says we need to be living as if the Chief Inspector will be showing up at any minute without notice. That's what he said when he wrote to the Thessalonians. He's going to show up unexpectedly, like a thief. A thief never calls you up and says, "I'll be over at six o'clock," does he? No, he shows up when he thinks you're not looking or not home.

Paul says we should be living as if Christ will come at any moment and starts out by saying, "And do this." What is the "this" that he is referring to? It goes all the way back to 12:1. "And do this...act as a living sacrifice." That means giving up and giving over to Jesus all that you are and have, including what you are able to do. It all should belong to the Lord, not to you.

It is an unchristian fallacy to think we should be working in this life to gain riches, wealth, and security. That's not a biblical concept. Those things may be given you by the Lord as a reward for faithfulness, but that is not what we should be working for. Our goal should be to earn enough to pay our family's basic expenses and some to share with others. Don't worry about your retirement plan. Don't worry about

Social Security down the road. It may not be there when you need it, and if it is, you know it's not going to be enough to live on anyway, so don't worry about it. Be faithful to God. Give everything over to Him.

He says in Matthew 6:33, "Seek first the kingdom of God and I will meet your basic needs." Do this then: give everything over to God including your whole life. Jesus said you should "love the Lord your God with all your heart, all your soul and all your mind."

Then he goes on to say, "Do this and be involved in ministry." Use your gifts, your talents, your time, your money, and the things you have possession of and control over. Use them for God. Use them for the ministry of reaching others with the gospel, for reaching the people who have needs like the children on the street, like the people who are struggling to survive, like the people who have never heard of Christ. Those in jail, those in nursing homes, and those in places where they can't help themselves all need you. These are all people who we should be helping.

That means if you have the ability to teach children, you should be teaching children. If you have a musical gift, you should be using that gift. Whatever your gift might be, use it for God. There are all kinds of ways you can work for God. Give it all over to Him.

By doing this, he says to show respect and honor to those in authority, no matter who you are, where you live, or under what kind of a government (chapter 13, the first few verses). Honor those in authority. Give them the respect they desire because God has placed them there for a reason. We might not understand it. We might not appreciate it. We might not act like that guy or that woman in authority because of the way they conduct themselves, because of their personality, or whatever reason. We should still respect them, honor them, and obey the laws, unless the law forbids evangelism. Do this, He says.

He goes on. Do this: show unconditional love to everyone. That kind of love that says I will accept you for who you are—a creation of God, loved by God, equal with me in the sight of God. You're not better than I am. You're not worse than I am. We are both sinners who need the saving grace of Jesus.

If you are a fellow Christian, you still need the love of Jesus, the guidance of the Scriptures, and the hope that we can have through Jesus. So, I'm going to love you. Like it or not, I'm going to love you anyway. You may not like me or the way I conduct my ministry. You may not even appreciate me, but I'm going to love you anyway because Jesus said I should and the Scriptures teach that I should.

Then we come to today's Scriptures. Do this, Paul says: do not live to satisfy your selfish desires. "Let us behave decently, as in the daytime not in orgies and drunkenness, not in sexual immorality and debauchery, not in dissention and jealousy." All six of these items that he mentions are selfish things. Things that people do when trying to please themselves, not anyone else. The list could be much longer. There are many other things that people do to please themselves. They buy fancy toys, big cars, boats, motorcycles, second homes, etc. trying to please themselves. In the end they feel miserable. The car breaks down. The camper roof falls in. The bank repossesses the boat or whatever. None of these things bring long-lasting satisfaction. The selfish desire that you try to please is never fulfilled.

You talk to people who are involved in sexual immorality, as Paul lists here, in orgies, in debauchery or all kinds of sexual pleasures, as they call it. Most of them will say, "I can't get enough." It becomes an addiction, a craving that is never satisfied. They end up with terrible diseases, a shortened lifespan, and they wish they could have avoided it all.

The same is true if we think of the financial focus that many people have. A little more is not enough. I got a 2% raise last year. This year I want 3%. I've $500,000 invested in a certain account; it should be a million by now. I need to change brokers. One Certificate of Deposit is paying a few percentage points more than another, let's switch banks. Let's get a little more.

What did Job say? "Naked I came into this world and naked I'm going to leave." Everything I've got is going to be taken away, so what's the point?

What is the point of trying to satisfy yourself with whatever it is that you're using to satisfy yourself? When you leave this world that satisfaction still will not have been met. Why not instead, Paul says, do this: show love for others. Try to satisfy others' needs. When you do that you will find true satisfaction because you know you are pleasing God as well as helping that other person.

Paul repeats this subject over and over, in not only this letter, but in almost every letter he wrote. Don't live for yourself. Live for God and the other person. The Apostle John said the same thing in his first letter toward the end of our Bible. There's a two-way relationship, he says. First, there should be an open relationship with God and an open relationship with your fellow man. You can have an open, loving relationship where you can gain strength from God and give to other people.

Paul says do this (verse 14): Put on the Lord Jesus Christ. When you get up in the morning and you've taken your shower, you go back to your closet and ask, What am I going to wear today? What determines your decision? Where you are going and what you're doing there. Whatever your plans are for the day, right? If you are going to work on a construction site you will choose the appropriate clothes for safety and comfort. If, however, you are scheduled to meet your banker or go to church, you would wear a different set of clothes.

So, when we get up in the morning, the first thing that should come to mind is: Thank you, Lord, for a new day. Lord, please get me through this day doing things that are pleasing to you. When I face today's challenges, give me strength. When I face the work I have to do today, give me wisdom. When I face decisions that have to be made today, may your Spirit guide me and teach me.

That's putting on Christ. That's getting ready for your day. That is equipping yourself for whatever life will throw at you. You need to do it every morning just like you get dressed for work, school or anything else. Put on the Lord Jesus Christ.

Do this, Paul says. These are the things we should be doing: acting sacrificially, being involved in ministry, showing respect and honor, showing unconditional love, living unselfishly and doing everything for the Savior under the power of the Lord Jesus Christ.

Why?

Do all these things while understanding the present

conditions we are living in. "Our salvation is nearer now then when we first believed," he says (verse 11). Now he did not mean our spiritual salvation. That comes by faith when we first trust Christ, when we first believe that Jesus is the Son of God and has risen from the dead for us. That is when we are saved spiritually. This term salvation he is using here is that stage when all our struggles are over and we are in the presence of God himself. We are saved from this world and all its temptations and influence. We are saved from all the struggles, the ridicule and the hardships we face in this life. That's over. We're saved from it now. We are in the presence of Jesus. We will soon be rescued from this life of evil, pain, and misery.

Paul said it's much closer now than it was when he first believed. Now Paul, by this time had been a Christian probably about four or five years. Some of us have been Christians for much longer than that. Paul declared that the return of Christ is much nearer now than when he first believed. How much closer is it now than then? We are very, very much closer.

We don't know when Christ will return, that is made very clear in Scripture. But for some reason God has delayed it until now at least. We don't know how much longer, but it doesn't matter. Every minute that goes by, every day that passes, we're closer to when he will return and the day our salvation is complete, the day we are taken out of this life of sinfulness, temptation and all the things that come with this life.

He says, "The night is nearly over. The day is almost here." A new day is dawning sometime in our near future, a day when Christ will come with a shout. The whole world will immediately change. All Christians will be taken out to be with Him and we will live with Him forever and ever. The rest of the world is left to its fate. The day is dawning. It is right on the horizon.

Some of us have, from time to time, stayed up all night. Maybe it was New Year's Eve, maybe it was an overnight fishing trip or something else. Maybe it was just for the experience. Along about 3:30 or 4:00 a.m. there is that anticipation. That knowledge that day is coming soon. The sun is going to rise. A new day will begin. Paul says that is where we're at right now. We're at that point where we know a new day is coming and it's going to be soon. If we're alive when it happens, we will welcome Jesus face to face. If we have already died, we will rise form the dead. We will come out of our graves to meet and greet Him.

It's there. It's waiting. "It's almost here," he says. For us who believe, it's a wonderful thing. When the sun shines it warms things up, makes things good and great. But over and over again in Scripture this is referred to as the Day of the Lord, and for those who don't believe or who reject the gospel of Jesus Christ, it's not going to be pretty. It's not going to be welcome. That will be a day of judgment. That will be a day when Christ sits on the throne and says to many people, "Depart from me, I never knew you."

So Paul says to do this: Live as if Jesus were coming today, this hour. Be ready for Him at all times because there won't be any time to clean up your act. Look forward to His coming. Don't try to please yourselves. Work for God. Work for others. When he shows up and greets you, He will say, "Well done, my good and faithful servant." You will be glad to stand before Him face to face.

Is there anything in your life that needs cleaning up? Do it now. The Lord may come at any time. Is there anything you should be doing you are not now? Get busy lest Jesus finds you slacking. Do these things on a regular basis, and there will be no need to panic when the trumpet sounds heralding his coming.

CHAPTER 27

Tolerance Without Compromise

Today's Bible Reading: Romans 14:1-15, 15:1-6

"We who are strong ought to bear with
the failings of the weak and not to please
ourselves. Each of us should please his
neighbor for his own good, to build him up"
—Romans 15:1, 2

Our American society today is being characterized as a society of tolerance. Politically, socially, and educationally, we are taught that we must learn to tolerate the differences in people, whether it be in lifestyle, religious beliefs, or ethnic teachings and practices. By tolerance it is meant that we should accept these differences in people with no desire or attempt to make any changes. We must accept them just as they are. It is the old philosophy of "live and let live."

This is not the basic teaching of Christianity. Christianity says we should accept people as they are, but through the power of Christ and the Holy Spirit, help them change into a people more like God.

Christianity says I will tolerate your areas of weakness, but at the same time I will help you grow spiritually. We all need to continually change. The very core of the Great Commission that Jesus gave at the end of his Gospels is based on this concept. He said to His disciples, "Go and teach them." That is, you need to present the gospel, first of all. Go and teach them. But he didn't stop there. He said also, "Make disciples." That means you have to teach them the principles of Scripture. Teach them what God expects from them once they ask Him to be their Lord and Savior.

Paul is saying here that people who are already Christians are not always on the same level spiritually. You cannot expect a new believer to be fully immersed, fully practicing, and to fully understand everything that's in Scripture. It's a fallacy or myth. Sometimes people who have been Christians a long time make the mistake of thinking everyone else knows as much as they do. It's simply not true.

When you try to ask people to practice things that you have found in Scripture that others haven't discovered yet, you might be forcing something on them they are not ready for. We shouldn't be doing that.

Paul starts off by saying we should not judge another Christian whose faith may be weaker than your own. Don't judge the man whose faith is weak. We as Christians need to stop doing that. We need to stop thinking that everyone else should be on the same level as I am and understand everything in Scripture the same way I do. Instead, we need to accept the fact that people are different. They understand at different levels, at different rates, and even sometimes come to different interpretations on minor issues.

If you have ever taken some kind of education course where you are being trained to teach other people, one of the very first things they tell you is that everybody learns at different rates and in different ways. That is a basic concept of educational philosophy.

I cannot walk into a group of second graders and teach them the same way I would a group of adults. It just wouldn't make sense. They are not ready for it. Even within the class of second graders there are bright students who catch on quickly and there are those students who need more personal help, more encouragement, or more time. People learn at different rates and in different ways.

It is the same way spiritually. People grow at different rates. We cannot expect a new believer to be a fully grown, fully immersed believer in the ways of God.

Paul, throughout his writings in the New Testament, makes this point several times. We need to be careful not to assume that everybody is maturing at the same rate. When he wrote to the young pastor Timothy, Paul gave him some examples of immature believers (1 Timothy 6:3-5).

Paul told Timothy there are people who love to argue over the finer points of Scripture. They take one word or phrase and build a big debate about it. He says we should avoid those kinds of people. Stay away from them. Don't get involved in those kinds of arguments.

If you remember back in the book of Acts, shortly after Paul was converted, he began going about teaching the resurrected Christ, the power of faith in Christ. Behind him came Apollos. Remember him? Apollos ends up in

Corinth about the same time as Paul. He is teaching Jesus Christ, but he is only teaching the Christ as presented by John the Baptist. "Christ is coming, get ready!" Apollos said. He didn't have the full understanding that Christ had already come and gone. He was an immature believer. He believed in Christ. He had faith in Christ, except it was not full or complete. So, he had to be corrected. He is just an example of an immature believer who may get involved in unhealthy debates.

Paul says in verse 14:1, to not pass judgment on people in disputable matters; matters that are separate from basic doctrines of Scripture. There are certain doctrines that are firm and unchangeable that must be believed and adhered to without compromise, but there are many other things in Scripture that are disputable or are minor points that won't make any difference to your salvation or anyone else's. Those are things he's talking about.

Paul uses two examples in this passage: one is holy days and the other is eating food. He says to not let that person who thinks that certain days of the year are special look down on you if you think every day is alike. Now if you think everyday is alike, don't think that other person is immature or wrong just because they like to celebrate the high holy days.

There are those churches that celebrate Advent and Lent for several days each year and have other high holy days on their calendar. That's fine and good if that's the way they want to practice their faith. It doesn't matter or affect their salvation or their relationship with God. In fact, for many people, they feel it draws them closer to God. Some people practice that every day is alike. "This is the day that the Lord has made. Let us rejoice and be glad in it." Yesterday was the same way. If the Lord tarries, tomorrow will be the same as well. Christ has come. He has been resurrected, and I will celebrate that every day. Paul's point is that both are equal in God's sight. It is a minor point whether we celebrate the high holy days or every day. That's something we should not be arguing about, nor judging someone if they do it differently from us.

He also talks about food. There are those who are strict vegetarians. They read the Scripture and think that God is telling them they should not eat meat. They are fully convinced of this. Other people read Scripture and say all food is fine. Whatever God provides, I will eat and be blessed by it. As long as I thank God for providing it for me all will be fine.

You remember from the first letter to the Corinthians, Paul had a similar argument. Some people were discussing whether or not they should buy meat from the market place if we know it has been sacrificed to idols. Paul said, I don't care where it comes from. As long as there is food on my table and I thank God for it, it's fine by me. But if I am invited to your house and you ask me to bring food with me and I know you are a vegetarian, it would be foolish of me to bring hamburgers, just because I like hamburger. If I know it's a problem for you to have meat on your table that you think was sold by a Buddhist, a Muslim, or someone of other faith, then I won't buy it there. I'll make sure I buy it from a Christian or some one of a similar faith as you. So when I show up I don't want to be the one that makes a stumbling block for you.

There are herbal teas available in stores produced by an

Eastern religious cult. I avoid them. But if you come to my house with a box of their tea I'm not going to offend you by refusing your gift.

That's what Paul is saying here. Be sensitive to their point of view. Don't put stumbling blocks in front of them. Don't make them feel as if you are judging them because of what they believe when this doesn't even matter. Paul says, I am fully convinced that all meat is equal and I can eat anything I want, but if I am going to my brother's house who feels differently, I am going to respect his beliefs on this matter because it doesn't affect our salvation. It doesn't affect our relationship with God at all.

Now I could go on with many other things. I am only about halfway through. Two more times in the letters of Paul, when he wrote to Titus, he said, "Avoid foolish controversies and genealogies and quarrels about the law, because it is unprofitable and useless." Another clear statement. Again, to Timothy in his second letter he said, "Don't have anything to do with foolish and stupid arguments (That's putting it right to the point.) because you know they produce quarrels and the Lord's servant must not quarrel. Instead he must be kind to everyone, apt to teach and not be resentful."

This brings up the second point that Paul makes with this lesson: we should accept people's differences within the body of Christ, understanding that not everybody matures at the same level and has not understood everything the same way we have. But what we need to be doing instead of arguing over the finer points, is working toward unity. We do that by accepting those differences and being careful not to impose on somebody else what you or I believe. Just because I believe a certain way does not mean everybody else has to on these minor issues. I'll give you just two quick examples.

Some churches practice the rite of baptism in different ways. Is it right or wrong to be immersed? Some people get into really heated arguments over this issue. I have done a thorough research on this subject, and my conclusion is that the Bible infers that it doesn't matter. I prefer immersion because it symbolizes what baptism is about, but in some cases you can use a different method. It will not affect your salvation.

In some churches, when you go to worship the people will practice different kinds of public prayer. In some churches the Pastor receives your requests and prays a few minutes over them. Other churches will issue a card in the bulletin and say if you have prayer requests, fill in the card and our staff will pray for you this week. They don't even have a public prayer for the people in the service. Some ignore it all together. They don't have anything like that at all, but that doesn't mean they don't pray.

Paul also makes the point that if we recognized that someone understands, practices, or sees things differently from ourselves, we should be ready to encourage them and teach them actually what Scripture says on that subject when they are ready to listen. That way we both learn. We both learn from Scriptures not from our own ideas. He tells us we know from the example of Apollos, that two of Paul's friends, when they found out what he was doing, took him and privately instructed Apollos in the truth regarding Christ. From that point on he taught the same way Paul did. He taught that Christ had already come and was resurrected and ready to receive people.

Paul says in this passage that we should be ready to teach and explain our points of view to others. Chapter 15:4 states, "Everything that was written in our past was written for our learning. So through the endurance of the Scriptures we might have hope." Everything we need to know is in there. If we have a question we should research it or have someone else research it so we can come to an understanding regarding what Scripture says on the subject. We should be ready to help another believer with that research with the idea that we are not going to try to change them to our point of view. Rather, we are going to let the Holy Spirit, through the Word of God, teach us both something. I might have to change my point of view. You might have to change yours. Some one else might have to change his point of view because of what the Scripture actually teaches.

In 2 Timothy 2:25, Paul finishes up when he wrote to that pastor. "The Lord's servant," he said, "must not quarrel. He must be able to teach." Then he goes on to say, "Those who oppose the Lord's servant, he (that is, the servant) must gently instruct in the hope that God will grant them repentance leading to a knowledge of the truth." So those of us who are more mature should be ready to reach out and teach the person who is weaker in his faith when he is ready to hear it. We should encourage him to search the Scriptures to build him up in his faith, not impose on him or pound into him what we think is right.

This is all done in the name of unity, in the name of love, so we can present a unified front to the world. Don't judge your fellow Christian. Accept him and help him to learn.

"Who are you to judge someone else's servant?" asks

verse 14:4. Those whom he is talking about are all servants of Christ, not each other. I'm not your master. You don't answer to me. Because I believe something should be done one way, I am not in a position to judge you because you do it in a different way. Paul says, "He will fall or stand to his own master, the Lord Jesus Christ."

Do you find yourself debating with a fellow Christian about things that are not related to salvation? Have you argued over points of discussion thinking you were right and someone else was wrong? What was the outcome?

We should always be going back to the Bible to find the truth about these kinds of things rather than trying to impose our beliefs on someone else. Let the Word of God speak for God.

CHAPTER 28

Neither Jew Nor Greek

Today's Bible Reading: Romans 15:7-13

"For I tell you that Christ has become a
servant of the Jews on behalf of God's
truth, to confirm the promises made
to the patriarchs so that the Gentiles
may glorify God for his mercy."
—Romans 15:8, 9a

The church at Rome was a multicultural church. People
came into the city from all over the known world. As a
result, the Christian church was made up of Jews, Arabs,
Turks, Greeks, and many other ethnic groups. When people
of various backgrounds get together for any common cause
or by a common bond, sometimes that common bond is
not always strong enough to overcome racism and prejudice.
In any society people of the same heritage tend to group
together. We've seen that here in America. People come
here and dwell in our largest cities creating neighbors like

Chinatown, Italian districts, and other such communities. It seems to be that an attachment to the common unit overrides any perceived need for blending into the established society.

Within the church of God, Paul says this should not be happening, even though we know from Scripture (Acts 2 and later) it was true right from the beginning. We also know from history and personal knowledge that it does. As far as Paul was concerned, what he is writing here in this letter to churches in a multicultural society like Rome and as we are, was that congregations should be made up of people who represent a variety of backgrounds but are fully accepted as equals. No racism. No prejudice. No distinction based on ethnic backgrounds.

That is not easy. In fact, it is one of the most difficult things people can do. To overcome such ingrained differences is not something we do naturally. But when we think about it we must realize that Christ has accepted anyone who comes by faith and so should we, no matter who they are, where they live, or what their background is. Christ said, "I love you, no matter who you are, and I love you in the condition you are in, and I want to take you and change you. Come to Me by faith."

The gospel message contains no race or ethnic restrictions. Think about what Jesus said in John 3:16, referring to the gospel of God. Did he say, "For God so loved the white people?" No. Did he say, "For God so loved the European people?" No. The Africans? No. He said, "For God so loved *the world* that he gave his only begotten Son." No exceptions. It is open to everyone.

We see this to be true immediately after the first church was formed. Christ had come and gone. He had gone back to the Father and left his commission to the Apostles. One of the first people God told Philip to speak to was a black man, the Ethiopian eunuch who was traveling through. The Spirit said, "Go, teach him what he's reading that he might understand the Gospel of God." So, black people were included in the early church and the gospel was taken to Africa.

We sing that old song, "Red and yellow, black and white, they are precious in His sight." Yes, everyone is precious, no matter who they are. Paul says at the beginning of this letter (1:16), "I am not ashamed of the Gospel for it is the power of God to salvation for everyone." Everyone. Not just the Jews. Not just white people. Everyone. The gospel message contains no racial or ethnic restrictions; therefore we should accept all people when they come to God by faith.

Now Paul has just been talking about showing love to your neighbor, showing true love, and he has discussed that subject both here and in 1 Corinthians. He said in both places that true love knows no racial or ethnic boundaries. So if someone is a Christian brother or sister we should love them, support them, and encourage them no matter who they are.

If a fellow Christian is in need we should be ready to rally around him, help him, support him, build him up and encourage him, give him the financial support if we can, and give him the physical support he needs, whatever it is without reservation.

Here in our part of the world we don't have the same kind of problems they have in other places. Our church is made up of all white people. That doesn't mean it will stay that way. Our church has in its community, people of other ethnic backgrounds. If they become Christians or come to us to worship with us, we should welcome them with open arms.

Other churches in our culture have a more mixed congregation, and some practice what Paul is teaching here better than others. Some do openly accept multicultural people and love them as they are. But, unfortunately, there are those who struggle with this problem even as the church at Rome was struggling when Paul wrote this letter to them.

The church at Rome had this divisive attitude of Jews versus Gentiles, and within those groups there were subgroups. They considered some better than others. Some were locals while others were from away. They had a struggle dealing with full acceptance.

There are churches in America that struggle with full acceptance. Recently someone told me about a church in the South which was planning an all church event such as a picnic or an outing. They were discussing what they would have on their menu for the meal. After discussing and deciding who would bring what and all that, one guy spoke up and said, "I suppose we ought to bring something for *them* as well." By *them* he was referring to the black people in his church. Brother, this ought not to be so. There ought not to be any kind of distinction. For those in the Southwest, the Mexican people are just as important to God as those born north of the border. The black people are welcome, the Italians are welcome, the Chinese, Japanese and every other people group are all welcome in God's new church.

In the church of God we cannot afford to have racism rampant in our church. Christ has accepted anyone, and we should accept them too.

We also should accept them because we know by experience and by fact that you cannot have true peace if there is prejudice in your heart. You know when you've offended someone. You know when you've violated a principle of Scripture. You know when God says this is wrong when you discriminate, ignore, or reject someone of a different race. You know your conscience is going to bother you, if you have any conscience at all. God gave you that conscience to remind you of what is right and good. That conscience will be exercised through the influence of the Holy Spirit to teach us when we are wrong and when we discriminate against people of other races.

Your conscience should bother you every time you have that feeling or attitude, every time you act on that attitude. The Holy Spirit should convict you and hold you accountable if you act that way because you're not showing true love. You're not really accepting that person as a brother or sister in Christ. True love says, "I welcome you as part of my family. I welcome you because God welcomes you."

Then your conscience will be clear and you can stand before God, knowing you have done right.

Neither Jew nor Greek. There is no distinction. There is neither male nor female, slave nor free. We are all one in Christ. We are all one in Christ by His grace, because it's His grace that brought us into His kingdom. It is His grace that keeps us and sustains us. It is His love, His power that keeps us, encourages us and teaches us to be one in the Spirit.

How do you react when you're around people of a different background? Do you find yourself thinking of them as being different? Do you sometimes wonder if they are of lesser value than yourself? Pray that the Holy Spirit will help you overcome those thoughts and treat each individual as a soul that Jesus loves and died for.

CHAPTER 29

A Missionary's Letter of Confidence

Today's Bible Reading: Romans 15:14-33

"I urge you, brothers, by our Lord Jesus
Christ and by the love of the Spirit, to join me
in my struggle by praying to God for me."
—Romans 15:30

What is your reaction when someone reads letters or notes from our missionary friends? I wonder if some of you, like I used to do, shut it out, just ignore it, and don't listen to what's being read.

What do you suppose the missionaries have in mind when they send those letters? Why do they even write to us anyway? Does it even matter to us what they're doing wherever they are? Do we need to know what is going on in Indonesia, Brazil, Africa or anywhere else? If we have a ministry here, should not our focus be here?

Well, as Paul closes out his letter to the church in Rome,

he makes three important notes to say it *is* important to listen to these letters. He, himself was a traveling evangelist who traveled all over the known world at that time. So he understood the situation from the missionaries' point of view. He knew what it was like to be out on the front lines and have people back at the established churches working locally. Perhaps as we look at what Paul says here it will give us a better sense of what goes on. It might make us more appreciative, more understanding, and more supportive of what people are doing in other places around the world.

Missionaries should have a strong sense of confidence in the churches that are sending them or helping to support them. He talks about three different aspects of that confidence in our text.

He starts out by saying, "I myself am convinced, my brothers, that you yourselves are full of goodness, complete in knowledge and competent to instruct one another." In other words, he is saying that a Christian missionary should be confident that the churches back home are spiritually healthy, not divided. Remember, he has already spoken throughout this letter on this subject of division from two or three different angles.

Recently, we just saw that he talked about the fact that there should be no prejudice or racism within the church. Earlier, he said there should be no division over theological matters. We should be united over what we believe and teach without arguing over the finer points.

He says that Christian missionaries should be confident that the people at home have a healthy spiritual church. I think he says that for two primary reasons. First, if a church is divided on any of these issues, whether it is theology, racism, prejudice or anything else, the attention or focus of the church will be on the issue at hand. It will be centered on the argument, disagreement, or discussion within the church. That is why we are instructed that if someone stirs up arguments or trouble within the church, he needs to be corrected. He needs to be dealt with and disciplined because if we are always spending time arguing, debating, and in discussion over such things, we are not spending time doing what God has asked us to do.

If the church's focus is on the internal issues, it will not have the time or make the effort to encourage, pray for, or really listen to people in other places.

So Paul says right off the bat that Christian missionaries should be confident that the churches at home are spiritually healthy. If a church is caught up in turmoil over internal things, it may also be divided over which missionary or agency deserves support. A church cannot support others spiritually if its own spiritual health is weak. It's impossible. That's also true of material support. How can we agree on whom to support and how much support they deserve if we cannot agree on the minor things within our own assembly? How can we agree if we are arguing and bickering over small points? Christian missionaries should have the confidence that people at home are united in their faith, in the Gospel and in their mission. That's why I think it is important enough to put right at the head of our church constitution the statement of our mission. This is what we stand for; this is what we are trying to do as a church. All members have to agree to that. Hopefully, we are working together to fulfill that mission.

People at home should be united and working together.

They should be spiritually healthy for mutual growth. Paul said, "I wrote to you quite boldly on some points because you needed to pay attention." You need to look at yourselves to see if you need to straighten out a little.

Then he goes on to say that Christian missionaries should be confident that supporting churches understand the missionaries' calling. Don't expect the missionary to do something he is not equipped to do or is not capable of doing. Paul says, "It is my mission 'to be a minister of Jesus Christ to the Gentiles'" We go back to the story of his conversion in the 9th chapter in the book of Acts. Very clearly, the person that God sent to him, to pray over him, to heal him of his blindness also delivered a message. "You, Paul, are a chosen vessel of God to minister to the Gentiles." Now Paul's heart, he told us earlier in this letter, was to his Jewish brethren. He said in one place, "I wish and I pray that all of my Jewish brothers were saved and became Christians. I know that this is not true and I know God has not called me to that mission, although I will not neglect them. I will still teach the Gospel when I am given the opportunity. My mission is to reach the Gentiles."

So if we receive a letter from missionary friends, wherever their ministry is located, we should not expect them to work with any group other than to those which they have chosen to focus. We should not expect translators to be hospital workers. We should not expect medical workers to be Bible teachers. We should recognize every missionary's calling to the task he is skilled or gifted to do.

It used to be when churches sent a missionary anywhere the concept given was that this person would go there and be a jack-of-all-trades. He would go to Timbuktu or some other remote place to minister. He would go there and be a teacher, a doctor, a pastor/missionary. He would be everything to everybody. Usually it ended up not working out very well. There were some converts. There were some beachheads made and established. Eventually, mission agencies caught on to this concept that Paul taught so many years ago. We need to be more specialized and more focused on the special gifts that each of us has. As a teacher, one missionary can influence her students, not only in the classroom, but outside as well. She can talk to them about the Lord and prepare them to receive Him and live for Him. We need to recognize that missionaries are called by God for specific missions and not think they are miracle workers who can do everything. It just isn't so.

That's true in our own lives, isn't it? I can't do everything. There are some things I certainly don't want to try to do, because I know I would mess it up. I'm sure you feel the same way about certain things. You're not comfortable or not equipped to do certain tasks, so you would be foolish to try them.

So, why should we think otherwise of our missionaries?

Paul also says of these missionaries that they have to be submissive to the leading and the working of the Holy Spirit through them. He, himself, says he was used by the Spirit and was empowered to give signs and miracles to prove his apostleship and to fight spiritual battles.

The first-century Christians, we know (especially the Apostles) had this gift. Beyond that we are not sure. God gave that gift to the early church in a world that might not necessarily have accepted Christianity without it. Signs, wonders and miracles were done through them.

There are miracles that happen today through some people whom God allows to act as agents. We should not put them down nor negate their ministry, but it's only where the Spirit wants to use them. We shouldn't think it to be true of every missionary. Some are gifted by God to perform miracles, some are not. Paul just thanked God that he was one of those who were given that privilege.

To sum up this point, we can simply say that missionaries are common people with a God given burden for a task that needs to be done, and they are able to do it. That's it.

The third point Paul makes (verses 27-33) is that Christian missionaries should be confident that supporting churches, the people back home, are praying for them and are willing to support them financially.

Over and over again in the letters we receive we hear the words, please pray for us. Please pray for so-and-so. Pray for this circumstance or that situation. Pray for what's going on. These missionaries understand the power of prayer.

Paul expresses it well when he says, "Join me in my struggles by praying for me," (verse 30). When we pray for somebody earnestly, faithfully, and specifically we are becoming a part of their work. We're helping that work, that ministry wherever it is and whatever they are doing. Praying for a missionary's child to get a legal passport is being a real part of that missionary's life. Entreating God on that child's behalf, I'm convinced, helps the process along. We are a part of their work when we pray for them.

We are also part of their work when we give them financial and material support. Paul talks about delivering the gift to the Jerusalem church by a couple of other area churches, the Macedonia and Achaia areas. Christians in those areas heard about the need of the mother church. The Christians in Jerusalem were struggling due to a localized famine at the time. The Macedonians and others said, "We're Christians too, and we have sufficient for our needs so we will help them out."

That's what we should be doing for every missionary that goes forth. It is a very sad thing to think that Christians have a calling by God and a burden to reach a particular group of people, given their gifts and skills, and then not be able to do it because they cannot afford to. Christian churches should be ready to rally around them, get behind them, and support them, prayerfully and financially.

In the past, our church has been very supportive of missionaries and does quite well in the area of prayer, encouragement and finances. We have sent boxes of goods which were really appreciated. The recipients knew they were gifts from our heart to support them in their work, in ways that were tangible, in ways that showed we cared. That's good. That's right.

Let's not fail to continue to do that, and when our missionary friends come home on furlough to visit with us, we should pray with them, we should encourage them, and send them away knowing they can keep their confidence in our church. We'll continue to stand behind them in all that they do wherever God has called them.

Have you prayed for a missionary this week? Do you know where missionaries supported by your church are serving? Do you know what they are doing? If you are not sure, it would be wise to check with your church leadership to find out so you, as an individual, can pray better for them and support them in other ways as your resources allow. Your church should also be making its people aware of the work and the needs of missionaries connected to your church. Your missionary friends need to have the confidence that you and your church stand behind them in the ministry God has called them to.

CHAPTER 30

Gaining a Worthy Reputation

Today's Bible Reading: Romans 16:1-27

"Now to him who is able to establish you
by my gospel and the proclamation of Jesus
Christ, according to the revelation of the
mystery hidden for long ages past, but now
revealed and made known through the
prophetic writings by the command of the
eternal God, so that all nations might believe
and obey him—to the only wise God be
glory forever through Jesus Christ. Amen."
—Romans 16:25-27

There's an old saying regarding public speaking that goes something like this: Say what you want to say, rephrase it and explain it or expand it, then say it again.

Well, when we look at the letter that Paul wrote to the church at Rome we find that he really uses the basis of that principle in this letter. If we go back to the first chapter, the eighth verse, we see Paul there, opening the letter by commending their faith. "First I thank my God, through Jesus Christ, for you because your faith is being reported all over the world." In other words, when he opened the letter he talked about the reputation of the church in Rome. Now, as he closes the letter, he is again talking about the reputation of the church among other believers and in the world, although he doesn't really talk about the world's opinion very much. Primarily he sticks with that of the believers. But he commended that church for having a reputation of being faithful to God in an ungodly world.

The bulk of the letter was written, as we have seen, to strengthen their faith even further, as a quick review of the outline would show. He reminded them of the basic truths of Christianity and how to put them into practice in daily life. Now he closes the letter with another reminder that everything we do within the church affects and influences what other people think of us. In other words, we build our own reputation.

More importantly than what other people think of us is what God thinks. Paul starts out in the first 16 verses of this chapter by talking about a reputation of welcoming fellow believers. He says, "I commend to you my sister Phoebe," then he goes on and gives a list of other people, that, if they should happen to come to Rome, he expects them to be welcomed into that church on the basis of his word. These are men and women who have worked hard in the Lord, people who are faithful to God wherever they are and whatever they're doing. He expected them to be welcomed because they are fellow believers.

When Christian leaders of other ministries recommend someone to us, we should take their word. We should welcome and accept people into our assembly, our church, our ministry based on their word. We should trust them that these people are faithful ministers of God who were working in other places.

It would be unwise for anyone responsible for filling a pulpit to go out and invite just whomever they pleased or recommend by some other source. But if a name is received that is recommended by another fellow believer that we know and trust to have sound judgment, that person should be welcome.

In our mobile society today, Christians move from church to church more frequently. That's an unfortunate characteristic of our society. When a Christian leaves this assembly or comes to this assembly, he should have with him letters of recommendation. The pastor or other church leaders should send those who move away or go to another ministry a note to the ministry where they are going stating that so-and-so is a faithful minister of the Lord and, as such, should be received without hesitation. That person would make a great asset to the new work to which he transfers. Every Christian should go on his way with a letter of recommendation.

Receiving churches should seek and ask for letters of recommendation. If a person comes in and says I am a Christian and I used to worship in such-and-such church, he should be asked pointedly concerning his previous experience.

There are three basic reasons why it is important to know a person's previous background. First, good godly people are not held back from ministering because the receiving church is waiting for them to prove themselves. If we get a recommendation from someone we can trust, we should welcome that person and allow him to get involved in the ministry right away.

Secondly, those who are running away from problems in their former church will be exposed. If you have a problem with a leader in your church and you move to another church to get away from it, that's not solving anything. That's not dealing with it, not resolving it, either between you and those leaders or between you and God, but it has to get settled.

Thirdly, selfish, ungodly people who are not true loyal workers of Christ will also be exposed. There might be something going on that might be more than a difference of opinion or in personalities. It might be a real problem with that person's relationship with God.

That's the second point that Paul makes in verses 17-20. "I urge you brothers to watch out for those who cause divisions," he says. Beware of those who stir up problems.

Not only should a church develop a reputation of welcoming fellow believers from other places, but we should also develop a reputation of being aware of false teachers, teachers who are in the ministry only for their own benefit, their own ego building, or for whatever they can get out of it.

I don't know how many times I have said this, and I will continue to say it: We are not in the ministry to please ourselves. We're in the ministry to serve others. The earlier and the quicker we get that straight, the better we will be and the better off everyone will be.

When a person's motive is self-promotion rather than having a Christ honoring ministry, then we'd better take note and take action. He says, you will need to be aware there will be false teachers, selfishly motivated people. When you discover them, take action. Keep away from them, and if it gets to the point where it creates division within the church, get them out of there. Take them out of positions of leadership and, if necessary, kick them out of the church entirely. You can't afford to have that kind of person in your church.

We need to be aware of false teachers who are selfishly motivated people.

Paul said in verse 19, "Everyone has heard about your obedience and I am full of joy over you. I want you to be wise about what is good and what is evil." Don't be naive, he says. Keep the faith. Stick to the Scriptures, but there will be people who will twist them and change them, so be careful.

Always stick to the Bible. If you stick to the Bible as your standard, as your rule book for life, you will soon weed out those unscrupulous people and God will be victorious. The God of peace will crush Satan under your feet.

Then he closes by saying we will gain a reputation among other believers and other churches as a church of faith and steadfastness. When a church develops a reputation, as we all do, everyone will know what kind of a church we are.

What kind of a church is yours? Every church that is active, every church that takes a stand in public on public issues or on doctrinal points of discussion gains a reputation. Is your church known as a liberal church, one that welcomes all interpretations of Scripture under one umbrella or is it a fundamental church that stands for certain doctrines without compromise? Is your church one that is open and warm and welcoming to believers and fellow worshippers or is it considered cold and reclusive?

I heard a story to illustrate this contrast about two churches. One was where a person went in to worship and was welcomed with open arms. Everybody there wanted to take him to lunch. They wanted to show generosity and love. At another church the experience was quite different. He walks in and sits down. No one even turns a head. When the service was over they all stood and filed out silently without even speaking to him. What kind of reputations do these two churches have in the mind of the visitor?

Is your church a church that is tolerant of people without compromise or is it considered bigoted and narrow? Are your people loud and boisterous in your services praising God to your full extent, worshipping God with your whole being, or are you quiet, serene and private in your worship? All these things help determine your reputation among believers. All these things say who you are and what you stand for.

How strong is our faith? What is our faith placed in and how firm is it? How do Christians in other places think of your local assembly? What is your reputation like? Is it as good as it might be or poor among those who know you? Those answers are important. We all should take care to develop good, godly, and faithful reputations.

But the closing statement in verses 25-27 is where the emphasis of this lesson lies. Paul has said, "I commend all these people to you and I warn you about some that might come in and be false teachers." I know you have a reputation among other believers, but this is the important thing: "Now to him who is able to establish you by my

Gospel and the proclamation of Jesus Christ...to the only wise God be glory forever through Jesus Christ."

It's what God thinks of you that counts in the long run. That's the most important thing. After all is said and done and you have discussed every issue mentioned in this open letter to the church at Rome, the central question is this: Are you faithful to God? Are you pleasing God with what you are doing and what you are as an individual and your assembly as a church? I pray that you are.

"To the only wise God be glory forever and ever. Amen."